Notting Hill Editions is an independent British publisher. The company was founded by Tom Kremer (1930–2017), champion of innovation and the man responsible for popularising the Rubik's Cube.

After a successful business career in toy invention Tom decided, at the age of eighty, to fulfil his passion for literature. In a fast-moving digital world Tom's aim was to revive the art of the essay, and to create exceptionally beautiful books that would be lingered over and cherished.

Hailed as 'the shape of things to come', the family-run press brings to print the most surprising thinkers of past and present. In an era of information-overload, these collectible pocket-size books distil ideas that linger in the mind.

www.nottinghilleditions.com

Alan Alexander Milne was born in London in 1882. He was educated at Westminster School and studied mathematics at Trinity College, Cambridge. He was a regular contributor to *Punch*, and later assistant editor, before the interruption of active service in the First World War. A remarkably versatile writer, Milne went on to become a hugely successful and widely-known playwright, both in the West End and on Broadway, as well as an essayist, poet, novelist and – most famously – children's author, as the creator of Winnie-the-Pooh. He died in 1956 following a long illness.

Frank Cottrell-Boyce is a children's novelist who won the Carnegie Medal for his first book *Millions* in 2004 and the Guardian Children's Fiction Prize for *The Unforgotten Coat* in 2013. *Millions* was made into a film by Danny Boyle, for whom Frank went on to work as the writer on the London Olympics Opening Ceremony, 2012. His other books include *Framed* (filmed by the BBC), *Cosmic*, *The Astounding Broccoli Boy* and *Runaway Robot*. His films include *24 Hour Party People*, *God on Trial*, *Hilary and Jackie*, and *Goodbye Christopher Robin* (2017), about the lives of A. A. Milne and his family.

HAPPY HALF-HOURS

–

Selected Writings of A. A. Milne

Introduced by
Frank Cottrell-Boyce

Notting Hill Editions

Published in 2020
by Notting Hill Editions Ltd
Mirefoot, Burneside, Kendal LA8 9AB

Series design by FLOK Design, Berlin, Germany
Cover design by Plain Creative, Kendal
Typeset by CB editions, London
Printed and bound
by Memminger MedienCentrum, Memmingen, Germany

This selection of A.A. Milne's articles was edited and arranged
by Roger Lewis

The essays and articles in this book have been reproduced by kind
permission of the Estate of the Late Lesley Milne Limited from the
following publications: *Not That It Matters* (1919); *If I May* (1920);
Those Were the Days (1929); *By Way of Introduction* (1929); *Peace with
Honour* (1934); *War with Honour* (1940); *Year In, Year Out* (1952)

A CIP record for this book is available from the British Library

ISBN 978-1-912559-05-3

www.nottinghilleditions.com

Contents

Frank Cottrell-Boyce

– Introduction –

How does a nation pull itself together again after a disaster? How do we move on from overwhelming experiences? There was no doubt in A. A. Milne's mind that the First World War was a disaster. On the Somme, he'd witnessed 'a lunacy that would shame the madhouse'. One Austrian Archduke had been killed, he said, and this 'resulted directly in the death of ten million men who were not archdukes'. Before the war he had been a star turn at *Punch* under the editorship of Owen Seaman. Seaman was a gloomy character who was partly the model for Eeyore. He was also an enthusiastic publisher and perpetrator of the kind of patriotic doggerel that cheered those ten million up the line to death. Milne was painfully aware of the part that culture played in soliciting sacrifice. 'Wars are fought for economic reasons,' he wrote, 'but they are fought by volunteers for sentimental reasons.' Seaman whipped up a lot of sentiment. Milne had been a pacifist since 1910. Seeing the Jingo-machine close up must have left a bitter taste. The pressure of it may have been partly why – despite his pacifism – he decided to sign up in 1915. Of course he didn't know then that this was only the first of the World Wars. He had every reason to believe that this was the War to End Wars

– a phrase that was coined by H. G. Wells, who sometimes played for the same cricket team as Milne. The Great War did not end all wars. But he learned that early on. In *The Honour of Your Country* he said that after the Somme 'all the talk in the Mess was of after-the-war'. He goes on to describe a conversation with a colonel whose 'idea of Reconstruction included a large army of conscripts'. The more Milne debates with him the more it becomes clear that nothing that happened on the Somme discredited the idea of war as a tool of diplomacy. The wittier Milne's responses become, the more obvious it is that war will continue to be part of the way we do things.

That cricket team he was in with Wells also included – at various times – J. M. Barrie, Kipling, Conan Doyle, P. G. Wodehouse, and G. K. Chesterton. It was Barrie who formed the team and named it the Allahakbarries, thinking he was playing with a phrase that meant 'God Help Us' – because he himself was such a bad player. So bad, in fact, that he banned the team from warming up at away grounds because the sight of them in action would only add to the opposition's confidence. In fact the phrase means 'God is Great' as you'll know from its appearance in various terrorist atrocities. The kind of violence Milne had witnessed does not go away.

In fact, Milne's 'after-the-war' was a streak of enormous luck. Despite seeing active and highly dangerous service as a signals officer, his later posting – on the

Isle of Wight – somehow left him time to start writing plays. His first was for the children of his colonel. He wanted to give them something amusing 'at a time when life was not very amusing'. Which is a decent enough mission for any writer. Certainly a better one than stirring up jingoistic sentiment (Milne's definition of a patriot was, someone who accuses other people of being unpatriotic). He moved away from *Punch*, ready to hit the West End running. As a successful playwright he would often earn £500 a week at a time when the average wage was about £4. He'd been lucky and he knew it. The American edition of his autobiography was actually called *What Luck*. The sense of being lucky gives the pieces he wrote about domestic life – about sorting out his books or redecorating the bathroom – the glow of unstated gratitude. He was lucky to have books to sort out. Lucky to be alive. Lucky to have got through the war without ever having to fire a shot in anger. Lucky therefore not to have had to compromise his pacificism.

Luck carries with it a sense of responsibility. Lucky survivors often feel they've been saved for some great purpose, or at least that they should make the most of their opportunity. You can sense this in how hard Milne worked to give those pieces their hospitable ease. Nothing is harder than making things look easy. If you read 'On Writing for Children' you'll see he had no patience for any writer who was 'not bothering'. Of a poem that was then a nursery favourite –

John Gilpin – he says 'there are sixty-three verses in it; it should have taken him a month of the hardest work within the capacity of man. When we read it, we know why it did not take him a month.' He was a fierce and fearless critic. In one very funny piece he takes a Sherlock Holmes story to pieces to demonstrate that it cannot be put back together again because it was only held together with chewing gum and sellotape. I don't think I've ever read a more insightful or bracing piece of criticism than his piece on Lewis Carroll and why the 'it was all a dream' ending is such a betrayal. His friend Frank Swinnerton said that Milne 'combined a gift for persiflage with the sternness of a Covenanter', and it shows in the sheer work ethic he brought to the task of making it look like he was doing nothing.

Of course no covenanter is going to be satisfied with 'merely' being amusing. One of the most moving and tortured pieces in this collection is 'The End of a Chapter', his account of why he has to stop writing about Christopher Robin. It's part excuse-note, part examination of conscience. He admits that Christopher Robin only got his name because the Milnes wanted their son to be a great cricketer and great cricketers – like W. G. Grace – have initials rather than names. He jokes about writer's jealousy of his own creation:

Imagine my amazement and disgust, then, when I discovered that in a night, so to speak, I had been pushed into a back place, and that the hero of *When We Were Very Young* was not, as I had modestly expected, the author, but a curiously-named child of whom, at this time, I had scarcely heard. It was this Christopher Robin who kept mice, walked on the lines and not in the squares, and wondered what to do on a spring morning; it was this Christopher Robin, not I, whom Americans were clamouring to see; and, in fact (to make due acknowledgement at last), it was this Christopher Robin, not I, not the publishers, who was selling the book in such large and ridiculous quantities.

Overwhelming success is harder to deal with than failure. At least failure has an element of hope in it. Success asserts a huge gravitational pull from which it's almost impossible to achieve escape velocity. Look how Conan Doyle struggled with Sherlock Holmes. How Steve Coogan keeps going back to Alan Partridge. How J. K. Rowling keeps returning to the Potter universe. Milne never returned. His refusal to dilute the legacy is partly why the colours of the Hundred Acre Wood are so fresh. He walked out of the trees, up to Galleon's Leap, and out into the World. Then he tried to stop a war.

The man who invented Winnie the Pooh said that the book he was most proud of writing was *Peace with Honour* – an anti-war polemic written in 1934. Nowadays, the whole idea of campaigning for appeasement in the 1930s has such a bad reputation that it's easy to forget that Milne was not the only one to argue against going to war with Nazi Germany. The book was a bestseller. You can feel how passionately he felt about this just by looking at the sheer rhetorical firepower he brings to the field. Scenes, sketches, aphorisms, statistics. It's a compelling read not least because Milne is genuinely wrangling with his conscience, trying to find a way of squaring his love of his country with his hatred of war. Of course by the time the true nature of Nazism became clear he had to renounce – or modify – his pacifism in the sequel to *Peace with Honour* – *War with Honour*. Clearly there's something ridiculous about performing such a flip-flop but you have to admire the honesty and the energy with which he tried to think through his change of mind. *War with Honour* is an angry, hectic book. Reading it is like watching a smartly-dressed gent desperately wrestling with a well-oiled snake, while trying to keep his tie straight. This is a book calling for peace in which the harshest words are aimed at Conscientious Objectors and the most hope is pinned on the atom bomb. 'The only logical protest for a Conscientious Objector who refuses to take part is suicide; preferably at sea, so that the war effort shall not be interrupted by the need for burying the body.' The atomic bomb on the other hand fills him with hope of a better world. Part of the thrill of the book is reading a man whose urbane voice normally comes at us from the nursery or the Garrick Club wrangling with an unusually apocalyptic version of nuclear deterrence. In the 1920s, he says, everyone was a pacifist. He talks about the optimism of the League of Nations and votes for women, for peace under the banner of hope. Here he is holding out for peace under the banner of planetary destruction. What Milne is really struggling with here is the clash between crisp clean principles and the murky, tempestuous nature of a fallen World. What can a writer bring to such a world?

Milne had already answered that with the Hundred Acre Wood. Children's books of the 1920s are thronged with children who never grow up, lead of course by Barrie's eternal Pan. But Christopher Robin is different. In the Hundred Acre Wood, Christopher Robin is the grown-up, dispensing wisdom and help, solving problems, putting things right. He's a boy at the very end of childhood, aware that this is soon going to end. That's why everything shimmers with its own transience. In the difficult, distracting, dangerous world into which he is heading when he walks beyond the wood (and in the end, the boy was off to another war), the best the writer can do is to bring the good things to our attention, to help us hold them in our hearts and memories, so that when we need them those little things – sorting out your books, picking a new bathroom, the honey and the humming – can be our stepping stones through the bad times. The joke in 'Vespers' is that the little boy who is supposedly praying is in fact distracted by everything from bath water to dressing gowns. But another way of looking at it, is to say that the boy was sure that everything from bath water to dressing gowns was important and had its place in the mind of God, or the universe. Everything matters. Everything in life is worth looking at. Milne's gift to write amusingly about the most trivial things is far from trivial. It's a kind of blessing. The kind that can put you back together again when all else fails.

LITERARY LIFE

– My Library –

When I moved into a new house a few weeks ago, my books, as was natural, moved with me. Strong, perspiring men shovelled them into packing-cases, and staggered with them to the van, cursing Caxton as they went. On arrival at this end, they staggered with them into the room selected for my library, heaved off the lids of the cases, and awaited orders. The immediate need was for an emptier room. Together we hurried the books into the new white shelves which awaited them, the order in which they stood being of no matter so long as they were off the floor. Armful after armful was hastily stacked, the only pause being when (in the curious way in which these things happen) my own name suddenly caught the eye of the foreman. 'Did you write this one, sir?' he asked. I admitted it. 'H'm,' he said noncommittally. He glanced along the names of every armful after that, and appeared a little surprised at the number of books which I hadn't written. An easy-going profession, evidently.

So we got the books up at last, and there they are still. I told myself that when a wet afternoon came along I would arrange them properly. When the wet afternoon came, I told myself that I would arrange them one of these fine mornings. As they are now, I have to look along every shelf in the search for the book which I want. To come to Keats is no guarantee that we are on the road to Shelley. Shelley, if he did not drop out on the way, is probably next to *How to be a Golfer though Middle-aged.*

Having written as far as this, I had to get up and see where Shelley really was. It is worse than I thought. He is between *Geometrical Optics* and *Studies in New Zealand Scenery.* Ella Wheeler Wilcox, whom I find myself to be entertaining unawares, sits beside *Anarchy or Order,* which was apparently 'sent in the hope that you will become a member of the Duty and Discipline Movement' – a vain hope, it would seem, for I have not yet paid my subscription. *What I Found Out,* by an English Governess, shares a corner with *The Recreations of a Country Parson*; they are followed by *Villette* and *Baedeker's Switzerland.* Something will have to be done about it.

But I am wondering what is to be done. If I gave you the impression that my books were precisely arranged in their old shelves, I misled you. They were arranged in the order known as 'all anyhow'. Possibly they were a little less 'anyhow' than they are now, in that the volumes of any particular work were at least together, but that is all that can be claimed for them. For years I put off the business of tidying them up, just as I am putting it off now. It is not laziness; it is simply that I don't know how to begin.

Let us suppose that we decide to have all the

poetry together. It sounds reasonable. But then Byron is eleven inches high (my tallest poet), and Beattie (my shortest) is just over four inches. How foolish they will look standing side by side. Perhaps you don't know Beattie, but I assure you that he was a poet. He wrote those majestic lines:

> The shepherd-swain of whom I mention made
> On Scotia's mountains fed his little flock;
> The sickle, scythe or plough he never swayed –
> An honest heart was almost all his stock.

Of course, one would hardly expect a shepherd to sway a plough in the ordinary way, but Beattie was quite right to remind us that Edwin didn't either. Edwin was the name of the shepherd-swain. 'And yet poor Edwin was no vulgar boy,' we are told a little further on in a line that should live. Well, having satisfied you that Beattie was really a poet, I can now return to my argument that an eleven-inch Byron cannot stand next to a four-inch Beattie, and be followed by an eight-inch Cowper, without making the shelf look silly. Yet how can I discard Beattie – Beattie who wrote:

> And now the downy cheek and deepened voice
> Gave dignity to Edwin's blooming prime.

You see the difficulty. If you arrange your books according to their contents you are sure to get an untidy shelf. If you arrange your books according to their size and colour you get an effective wall, but the poetically inclined visitor may lose sight of Beattie altogether. Before, then, we decide what to do about it, we must ask ourselves that very awkward question, 'Why do we have books on our shelves at all?' It is a most embarrassing question to answer.

Of course, you think that the proper answer (in your own case) is an indignant protest that you bought them in order to read them, and that you put them on your shelves in order that you could refer to them when necessary. A little reflection will show you what a stupid answer that is. If you only want to read them, why are some of them bound in morocco and half-calf and other expensive coverings? Why did you buy a first edition when a hundredth edition was so much cheaper? Why have you got half a dozen copies of *The Rubáiyát*? What is the particular value of this other book that you treasure it so carefully? Why, the fact that its pages are uncut. If you cut the pages and read it, the value would go.

So, then, your library is not just for reference. You know as well as I do that it furnishes your room; that it furnishes it more effectively than does paint or mahogany or china. Of course, it is nice to have the books there, so that one can refer to them when one wishes. One may be writing an article on sea-bathing, for instance, and have come to the sentence which begins: 'In the well-remembered words of Coleridge, perhaps almost too familiar to be quoted' – and then one may have to look them up. On these occasions a library is not only ornamental but useful. But do not let us be ashamed that we find it ornamental.

Indeed, the more I survey it, the more I feel that my library is sufficiently ornamental as it stands. Any reassembling of the books might spoil the colour-scheme. *Baedeker's Switzerland* and *Villette* are both in red, a colour which is neatly caught up again, after an interlude in blue, by a volume of Browning and Jevons' *Elementary Logic.* We had a woman here only yester-day who said, 'How pretty your books look,' and I am inclined to think that that is good enough. There is a careless rapture about them which I should lose if I started to arrange them methodically.

But perhaps I might risk this to the extent of get-ting all their heads the same way up. Yes, on one of these fine days (or wet nights) I shall take my library seriously in hand. There are still one or two books which are the wrong way round. I shall put them the right way round.

– Children's Books –

There is a well-established belief among uncles that all babies like to listen to the tick-tick. Perhaps they do. After all, for the first twelve months of one's life there isn't, in the way of spiritual refreshment, very much else that offers. One either listens to a watch ticking or one listens to it not ticking. So the millionth uncle takes out his gold hunter and says complacently, 'Hark to the tick-tick'; the millionth baby is presumed to be harking; and, since no comment is made, the legend that he likes harking goes irresistibly on. The ideal baby-entertainer is the man with the watch.

In something the same way the 'children's writer' has established himself. To a child of age to read, or to be read to, any book is better than no book, to which extent any book is a children's book. And because, I suppose, the first 'children's writer' wrote in a certain way, as being the easiest way in which to write, a certain sort of book came to be regarded as the ideal children's book, and it was agreed that the writer of any such book might safely be referred to as one who understood completely the psychology of the child's mind.

'Being the easiest way in which to write.' That is the secret of nine-tenths of the Christmas Books – now so many that they demand a supplement to themselves. Inasmuch as the average father stops being a solicitor or a stockbroker (jobs at which he is an expert) in order to become, for the amusement of his child, an extremely indifferent actor, novelist or draughtsman, so is it assumed that, even in the more formal making of a book, this amateurishness, this sense of relaxation, is not only 'good enough' for a child, but is, in a way, a kind of guarantee that one really is amusing the kid, rather than exhibiting oneself priggishly, in one's own special line, as an expert. For, seeing the author so much at his ease, nobody can fail to realize that he is writing 'for the young', and not, the selfish cad, for himself.

Let us begin a story for children and see where it leads us.

'Once upon a time there was a little girl called – well, you will never guess what her name was, not if you had three hundred million guesses, and your Daddy and your Mummy and your Nanny all guessed too, and you read the Englishdictionary (isn't that a long word?) right through from beginning to end, including all the twiddly-widdly bits. Because she had a special name of her very-very-very-own, which nobody had ever been called before, and it wasn't Mary, and it wasn't Jane, and it wasn't Anne, and you'll never believe it but it wasn't even Flibberty-gibbet. What *could* it have been? Can't you guess? Not even if you hold your thumbs tight, and shut your eyes, and take your very very deepest breath like you do when you're not-feeling-very-well-this-morning-Nanny, and the doctor-man comes and tells you to say 'Ninety-nine'? Well, then I shall have to tell you. Her name was Yesterday. Isn't that a funny name?'

It is not unfair to take this as a representative sample of the children's-story manner. You see the advantage of it. So far the author has told us that there was once a little girl called Yesterday; a matter of eight words and a certain amount of invention. Without taxing his inventive powers any further, he has written a hundred and seventy words, and is still going strong. As I have said, it is the easiest way in which to write. There is nothing to stop you. You can go on and on at your ease, with your waistcoat unbuttoned *(mutatis mutandis,* if you are a woman), confident that the little ones are enjoying it.

Let us turn to poetry and consider a supreme example of relaxation: *John Gilpin, or, The Curate Unbends.* It is not a typical 'children's poem', though it has been sold often enough as 'suitable for a child', but it is typical of the method. Cowper was a poet; he wrote *The Task*; took it seriously, we may suppose, from ten till two each morning; but *John Gilpin* was another matter. He had been told the story by Lady Austen. It was a humorous story. One must not blame him for supposing that, if he turned it into verse, the result would inevitably, one might almost say legally, be humorous verse. At any rate it would not be serious verse, and therefore need not be taken seriously, not even by the author. 'So he jotted it down' during a 'sleepless night'. There are sixty-three verses in it; it should have taken him a month of the hardest work within the capacity of man. When we read it, we know why it did not take him a month.

> Quoth Mrs. Gilpin, 'That's well said;
>   And for that wine is dear,
> We will be furnished with our own
>   Which is both bright and clear.'

'Why "bright and clear"?' you ask. 'Why not?' answers Cowper. 'It helps to end the line and rhymes with "dear".'

> He soon replied, 'I do admire
>   Of womankind but one.'

Why 'soon replied' when he obviously answered at once; why 'I do admire', when he would naturally say 'I admire'? 'Well,' says Cowper, 'you have to have eight syllables in the line, and as I only had six, I put in two more. It still makes grammar.'

I fancy that in verse, even if written for the young, there should be something more than grammar, the correct number of syllables in a line, and correct rhymes at prearranged intervals. If I write:

When Tommy saw his dog again,
  A cry he then did give,
And took him quickly back to where
  They both of them did live

– if I write this, it can only be because I am not bothering. Instead of spending days at it, I am working off
my sleepless nights. How many children's books, one
wonders, are the result of sleepless nights – the days, of
course, being devoted to 'serious' work?

This brings us back to the old question, What
do children like? The answer to the question con-
cerns the writer for children as much as, and no more
than, the answer to the question 'What do men and
women like?' concerned Shakespeare or Dickens. In
other words – and I have taken a long time coming
to the obvious – a 'children's book' must be written,
not for children, but for the author himself. That the
book, when written, should satisfy children must be
regarded as a happy accident, just as one regards it as
a happy accident if a dog or a child loves one; it is a
matter of personality, and personality is the last matter
about which one can take thought. But whatever fears
one has, one need not fear that one is writing too well
for a child, any more than one need fear that one is
becoming almost too lovable. It is difficult enough to
express oneself with all the words in the dictionary at
one's disposal; with none but simple words the difficulty is much greater. We need not spare ourselves.

This, I think, is the one technical concession which must be made: the use of simple words. It is, of course, annoying when your second line ends in 'self' to realize suddenly that you are writing a 'children's book' and mustn't say 'pelf'; many a poet has torn up his manuscript at this point and started on a sex novel, as giving him more scope. Others have said 'pelf' and not bothered. They are the ones who dash off their poems during a sleepless night, thinking anything good enough for a child. But those who are themselves still children as they write will reject 'pelf' instinctively, as one of those short cuts which spoil the game. It makes writing more difficult; amazingly so, at a moment when we were hoping to relax a little from the serious work of describing Life in the Night Clubs, but alas! there seems to be no help for it.

– Lewis Carroll –

To turn to another sort of writing. Charles Lutwidge Dodgson was born on January 27th, 1832, became a mathematical lecturer at Oxford in 1855, and was ordained deacon in 1861. Mathematical lecturers joke with difficulty; clergymen with lamentable ease. The combination does not seem promising. We picture Don Dodgson and Deacon Dodgson setting out together to amuse the Liddell girls, and for all the brightness of the day we shudder. But this was one of those enchanted afternoons when anything may happen. A fairy wand touched Don and Deacon, and magically they became Lewis Carroll; the three little girls became magically a million little girls, a million little boys, big girls, big boys, men and women; and there was born on a golden afternoon nearly ninety years ago Alice, of Wonderland and the Looking Glass. But don't suppose that this strange Lewis Carroll was now trying to amuse a world-audience, or that he was thinking, when once he had put pen to paper, of his Liddell girls. He was writing solely to amuse the strange Lewis Carroll, this childlike person whom he had suddenly discovered in himself. Sometimes one of the old Dodgsons would elbow his way in and insist on being amused too. Then would come prolonged aquatic jokes about 'feathering' and 'catching crabs', such as would appeal to an unathletic deacon and be the occasion of sycophantic laughter from a nice little girl.

Turn to the 'Wool and Water' chapter in the *Looking Glass,* and listen carefully to the conversation between the Sheep and Alice in the boat. The Reverend Dodgson is at large. Turn to the next chapter and listen to Humpty Dumpty:

'When I use a word,' Humpty Dumpty said in rather a scornful tone, 'it means just what I choose it to mean – neither more nor less.'

'The question is,' said Alice, 'whether you can make words mean different things.'

'The question is,' said Humpty Dumpty, 'which is to be master – that's all . . . Impenetrability! That's what *I* say.'

Lewis Carroll is back again. The Deacon has vanished with the suddenness which is such a feature of the country.

But it must have been the Don who insisted afterwards on making the stories into dreams.

'My dear fellow,' he said to Carroll, 'a human child couldn't go down a rabbit-hole. Consider for a moment the relative sizes of the aperture and the intruding body. And, in any case, rabbits do not talk, and what's all this about substituting a flamingo for a croquet-mallet? Have you ever observed the Common

Flamingo – *Phoenicopterus Antiquorum?* Think carefully for a moment and you will see that the whole thing is absurd. Now, if it had been Alice's *dream* – well, we all know what ridiculous things happen in dreams. Only last night I dreamed that I was giving a lecture on Determinants in my night-shirt, before, of all people, the late Prince Consort, when suddenly –

And Lewis Carroll rubbed his head in a bewildered way and said sadly, 'No, it couldn't have happened, could it? You know, just for a moment I thought it did. Somewhere . . . somehow . . . Oh, well.' So it became (how wrongly, how stupidly) a dream and, being a work of genius, managed to survive it.

For who is ever interested in somebody else's dream? Do we think of Alice as a little girl who ate too much pudding for dinner and had a nightmare in the afternoon? We can all do that for ourselves.

But Alice is that real little girl who, alone of all little girls, has had tea with the March Hare and the Mad Hatter, and played croquet with the Queen of Hearts; who has had 'Jabberwocky' explained to her by Humpty Dumpty, and heard Tweedledee recite 'The Walrus and the Carpenter'; the child who walked into the setting sun by the side of the White Knight, that gentle, foolish, fond old man, with whom, in some literary Valhalla, Mr Dick flies kites – special kites, kites not now of Mr Dick's invention.

'I was wondering what the mouse-trap was for,' said Alice. 'It isn't likely that there would be any mice on the horse's back.'

'Not very likely, perhaps,' said the Knight, 'but if they *do* come, I don't choose to have them running all about.'

O happy Carroll! O blessed Knight! Did Alice dream that? Listen:

Years afterwards she could bring the whole scene back again, as if it had been only yesterday' – the mild blue eyes and kindly smile of the Knight – the setting sun gleaming through his hair and shining on his armour in a blaze of light – the horse quietly moving about, with the reins hanging loose on his neck, cropping the grass at her feet – and the black shadows of the forest behind.

There you have Lewis Carroll giving the lie to the Dodgsons. It was no dream, no story for children. It happened. He was there himself.

I have emphasized the absurdity of the dream-convention, because it is Alice who has kept the books in the hearts of children, Alice of whom children would expect real adventures, not dreams. But it is also Alice who was responsible for the occasional intrusions of the Dodgsons: the chop-logic of the Don, the over-easiness of the Deacon. They never could resist a little girl. In *The Hunting of the Snark* there is no little girl, and the result is undiluted Carroll, the most inspired nonsense in the language. Had he written no more than the *Snark* and *The Walrus and the Carpenter,* he would have deserved immortality.

But he would not have got it. He needed Alice to hold his hand. She is not pretty, as drawn by Tenniel; she has no great charm of manner; but, because she is a real child, wherever her piping voice is heard, children will follow, and at their heels will troop the grown-ups, eager to see what strange new company she is keeping. Look! Now she is talking to a man on a horse! Observe the spiked anklets round the horse's feet. That is to guard against the bites of Sharks. It is the rider's own invention . . .

– The Robinson Tradition –

Having read lately an appreciation of that almost forgotten author Marryat, and having seen in the shilling box of a second-hand bookseller a few days afterwards a copy of *Masterman Ready*, I went in and bought the same. I had read it as a child, and remembered vaguely that it combined desert-island adventure with a high moral tone; jam and powder in the usual proportions. Reading it again, I found that the powder was even more thickly spread than I had expected; hardly a page but carried with it a valuable lesson for the young; yet this particular jam (guava and cocoanut) has such an irresistible attraction for me that I swallowed it all without a struggle, and was left with a renewed craving for more and yet more desert-island stories. Having, unfortunately, no others at hand, the only satisfaction I can give myself is to write about them.

I would say first that, even if an author is writing for children (as was Marryat), and even if morality can best be implanted in the young mind with a watering of fiction, yet a desert-island story is the last story which should be used for this purpose. For a desert-island is a child's escape from real life and its many lessons. Ask yourself why you longed for a desert-island when you

17

were young, and you will find the answer to be that you did what you liked there, ate what you liked, and carried through your own adventures. It is the 'Family' which spoils *The Swiss Family Robinson*, just as it is the Seagrave family which nearly wrecks *Masterman Ready*. What is the good of imagining yourself (as every boy does) 'Alone in the Pacific' if you are not going to be alone? Well, perhaps we do not wish to be quite alone; but certainly to have more than two on an island is to overcrowd it, and our companion must be of a like age and disposition.

For this reason parents spoil any island for a healthy-minded boy. He may love his father and mother as fondly as even they could wish, but he does not want to take them bathing in the lagoon with him – still less to have them on the shore, telling him that there are too many sharks this morning and that it is quite time he came out. Nor for that matter do parents want to be bothered with children on a South Sea holiday. In *Masterman Ready* there is a horrid little boy called Tommy, aged six, who is always letting the musket off accidentally, or getting bitten by a turtle, or taking more than his share of the cocoanut milk. As a grown-up I wondered why his father did not give him to the first savage who came by, and so allow himself a chance of enjoying his island in peace; but at Tommy's age I should have resented just as strongly a father who, even on a desert-island, could not bear to see his boy making a fool of himself with turtle and gunpowder.

I am not saying that a boy would really be happy for long, whether on a desert-island or elsewhere, without his father and mother. Indeed it is doubtful if he could even survive, happily or unhappily. Possibly William Seagrave could have managed it. William was only twelve, but he talked like this: 'I agree with you, Ready. Indeed I have been thinking the same thing for many days past . . . I wish the savages would come on again, for the sooner they come the sooner the affair will be decided.' A boy who can talk like this at twelve is capable of finding the bread-fruit tree for himself. But William is an exception. I claim no such independence for the ordinary boy; I only say that the ordinary boy, however dependent on his parents, does like to pretend that he is capable of doing without them, wherefore he gives them no leading part in the imaginary adventures which he pursues so ardently. If they are there at all, it is only that he may come back to them in the last chapter and tell them all about it . . . and be suitably admired.

Masterman Ready seems to me, then, to be the work of a father, not of an understanding writer for boys. Marryat wrote it for his own children, towards whom he had responsibilities; not for other people's children, for whom he would only be concerned to provide entertainment. But even if the book was meant for no wider circle than the home, one would still feel that the moral teaching was overdone. It should be possible to be edifying without losing one's sense of humour. When Juno, the black servant, was struck by lightning and not quite killed, she 'appeared to be very sensible of the wonderful preservation which she had had. She had always been attentive whenever the Bible was read, but now she did not appear to think that the morning and evening services were sufficient to express her gratitude.' Even a child would feel that Juno really need not have been struck by lightning at all; even a child might wonder how many services, on this scale of gratitude, were adequate for the rest of the party whom the lightning had completely missed. And it was perhaps a little self-centred of Ready to thank God for her recovery on the grounds that she could 'ill be spared' by a family rather short-handed in the rainy season.

However, the story is the thing. As long as a desert-island book contains certain ingredients, I do not mind if other superfluous matter creeps in. Our demands – we of the elect who adore desert-islands – are simple. The castaways must build themselves a hut with the aid of a bag of nails saved from the wreck; they must catch turtles by turning them over on their backs; they must find the bread-fruit tree and have adventures with sharks. Twice they must be visited by savages. On the first occasion they are taken by surprise, but – the savages being equally surprised – no great harm is done. Then the Hero says, 'They will return when the wind is favourable,' and he arranges his defences, not forgetting to lay in a large stock of water. The savages return in force, and then – this is most important – at the most thirsty moment of the siege it is discovered that the water is all gone! (Generally a stray arrow has pierced the water-butt, but in *Masterman Ready* the insufferable Tommy has played the fool with it. He would.) This is the Hero's great opportunity. He ventures to the spring to get more water, and returns with it – wounded. Barely have the castaways wetted their lips with the precious fluid when the attack breaks out with redoubled fury. It seems now that all is lost . . . when, lo! a shell bursts into the middle of the attacking hordes. (Never into the middle of the defenders. That would be silly.) 'Look,' the Hero cries, 'a vessel off-shore with its main braces set and a jib-sail flying' – or whatever it may be. And they return to London.

This is the story which we want, and we cannot have too many of them. Should you ever see any of us with our noses over the shilling box and an eager light in our eyes, you may be sure that we are on the track of another one.

– Oscar Wilde –

The last two acts of *The Importance of Being Earnest* are set in The Manor House, Woolton, Hertfordshire, the country home of Mr John Worthing. For the encouragement of British Railways I propose to examine the train service which the village of Woolton enjoyed in 1894 under private enterprise.

The first arrival from London on this July afternoon is Algernon Moncrieff, nephew of Lady Bracknell. Internal evidence allows us to put the time at 3.30. He is followed by John Worthing, who arrives about seven minutes later (3.37); by the Hon. Gwendolen Fairfax (3.58); and by her mother, Lady Bracknell (4.28). Since each of these four was related to, or an old friend of, the others, and was greatly surprised by their arrival, it is clear that they came by different trains. Lady Bracknell, indeed, announces that she followed her daughter 'at once by a luggage train'. This seems a little capricious of her. With three passenger trains arriving within half an hour, it is unlikely that she would have had long to wait for a fourth. As it is, we can but admire the unusual speed of the G.N.R.'s goods service, and the elasticity which allowed her ladyship to travel by it.

Now three Down trains and a goods train arriving

at a small country station within the hour is well enough; though not enough, perhaps, to impress any but the regular users of small country stations. But we must remember that other trains may have been flowing in at short intervals conveying other passengers than those destined for The Manor House. Indeed, to judge from the Up service, they must have been pouring in. At about 4.35 Lady Bracknell looks at her watch and says 'Gwendolen, the time approaches for our departure.' A little before 4.45 she looks at her watch again, and says, 'Come, dear, we have already missed five, if not six, trains.' Even accepting the lower estimate we can still admire the almost reckless enthusiasm of the Great Northern Railway. Today my own country station offers nothing between 3.13 and 5.14. However, as the 3.13 takes just over three hours to cover 36¾ miles, and the 5.14 just under two hours, it is perhaps as well that we are exposed to no further temptation.

It is, I suppose, possible that some dogged Public Relations Officer, wishing to do what he can for nationalization, will now point out that *The Importance of Being Earnest* is a work of the imagination, and that the train service to an imaginary village in it cannot legitimately be compared with that provided so efficiently by British Railways. If so (and it would be very unromantic of him) he will merely shunt me on to another line. I shall now invite the innocent public, which knows so little and cares so little about the troubles of a writer, to consider how the passing years have removed, or added to, those troubles.

Wilde wanted to get four people from London to The Manor House, Woolton, so that they arrived at four different times between 3.30 and 4.30. There was only one way of bringing them there – by train. Had this been what is called a serious play, he would have been criticized severely for his indifferent crafts-manship and his poor sense of reality. Today, how easy! Any character can arrive anywhere at any time, dependent only on his own whim and that of the author. Any number of people can start from London at the same time, if that be necessary to the plot, and arrive as required at any Manor House in any county. They can start at different times, and enter, should the situation demand it, dramatically together. They have driven down, and the horse-power of their cars, or the speed-lust of the drivers, is of no moment to anybody. No explanations are asked for or expected. Add to the motor-car the telephone, and the modern dramatist is seen to be on velvet, or in clover, whichever he prefers.

LADY MARY (*in the middle of triangular drama*): I think it would be as well if my solicitor were here. He lives at the other end of the Cromwell Road, but he has a fast car. If you will excuse me, Mrs Fortescue, I will ring him up.

(She goes out, thus giving George and Mrs Fortescue the short, passionate love-scene which the audience was beginning to wonder if it would get. Without the bites it would look nothing in print, and we shall therefore leave it out. Lady Mary returns.)

GEORGE: Is he coming?

LADY MARY: By a fortunate chance, he had only just reached home, so that his car was already at the door. He will be here at any moment. (*A bell rings.*) Ah, there he is.

– Introducing Shepard –

There are other differences between Author and Artist than the medium of expression. For instance, an artist of reputation who illustrates advertisements of soap is an object of nothing but envy to his fellows, whereas a writer of similar reputation, who had been exposed as the author of such delightful dialogues as precede the arrival of furniture in plain vans, would deem it necessary to slink past Sir Edmund Gosse with his hat over his eyes. Why this is so I cannot say; nor why, when an author produces a book entirely on his own, no artist is asked to write an introduction, whereas the book of Shepard cannot make its charming bow to the world until Milne, or somebody moderately respectable, has agreed to chaperon it.

Mr E. H. Shepard, of all people, needs no introduction at my hands. Anybody who has heard of me has certainly heard of Shepard. Indeed, our names have been associated on so many title-pages that I am beginning to wonder which of us is which. Years ago when I used to write for the paper of whose staff he is now such a decorative member I was continually being asked by strangers if I also drew the cartoons. Sometimes I said 'Yes.' No doubt Mr Shepard is often asked if he wrote 'The King's Breakfast'. I should be proud if he admitted now and then that he did.

I must confess that I am writing this Introduction a little self-consciously; feeling, no doubt, much as Mr Elliott feels when asked to photograph Mr Fry. We have a perfectly true story in our family that one of us was approached by an earnest woman at some special function with the words, 'Oh, are you the brother of A. J. Milne – or am I thinking of Shepperson?' E. H. Shepard, though surely he owes something to that beautiful draughtsman, is not to be mistaken for Claude Shepperson, nor am I that other, to me unknown, from whom I have so lamentably failed to profit; but you see what she meant. You see also what I mean; and how I am hampered by the fear that somebody may read this Introduction, and feel that Mr Shepard is not being very modest about himself. For if I let myself go I could make him seem very immodest indeed.

Perhaps this will be a good place in which to tell the story of how I discovered him. It is short, but interesting. In those early days before the war, when he was making his first tentative pictures for *Punch*, I used to say to F. H. Townsend, the Art Editor, on the occasion of each new Shepard drawing, 'What on earth do you see in this man? He's perfectly hopeless,' and Townsend would say complacently, 'You wait.' So I waited. That is the end of the story, which is shorter and less interesting than I thought it was going to be.

For it looks now as if the discovery had been somebody else's. Were those early drawings included in this
book, we should know definitely whether Townsend
was a man of remarkable insight, or whether I was just
an ordinary fool. In their absence we may assume fairly
safely that he was something of the one, and I more
than a little of the other. The Shepard you see here is
the one for whom I waited; whom, in the end, even I
could not fail to recognize.

Art is not life, but an exaggeration of it; life
reinforced by the personality of the artist. A work of
art is literally 'too good to be true'. That is why we
shall never see Turner's sunsets in this world, nor
meet Mr Micawber. We only wish we could. But Life
does its best to keep the artist in sight. Whether sunsets tried to be more Turneresque in the 'fifties I do
not remember, but the du Maurier women came in a
stately procession well behind du Maurier, and bant-
ing youth toils after Shepperson in vain. Kensington
Garden children are said to be the most beautiful in
the world, but in a little while Shepard will make them
more beautiful than ever. Bachelors remain bachelors because they are always just a little too late for
the fair, their adoration having shifted with the years
from the du Maurier girl to the Gibson girl, and from
the Gibson girl to the Baumer girl, until bachelordom
was a habit. But every mother prays simply for a little
Shepard child, and leaves it to Mr Shepard whether it
is a boy or a girl. . . .

Which reminds me that, whether anybody else or not is liking this introduction, Mr Shepard himself is beginning to feel anxious about it. However modest we are in public, in private we are never too modest for praise; but we do like to be praised for the right thing. Mr Arnold Bennett will remain unmoved if you tell him that he knows all about the Five Towns, but he will blush delicately if you assure him that he knows all about Town. So with the rest of us. No artist but hates to be pinned in a groove like a dead and labelled butterfly, and none of the secular but loves so to pin him, feeling that thus, and only thus, is he safe. Not many of the pictures here are pictures of children, but I can imagine Mr Shepard saying wearily, when their legends were sent to him for illustration, 'Children again! But I can *do* children! Give me something I'm not so sure about, like the inside of a battleship or a Bargee's Saturday Night.' Well, here are some of the others; nor battleships, nor bargees; but not children. For in a sense this book is Mr Shepard's escape from me, and from the setting-board to which I have selfishly condemned him. How unfortunate that, even here, I am at his elbow. 'Ah! Drawings of children,' some fool will say, seeing our names together on the title-page. But he will be wrong. They are just drawings of Shepard's.

My one regret is that there are still no bargees. Not because, as some dull people seem to think, only the slow, the insensitive, and the unimaginative are proper subjects for a work of art, but because a Shepard bargee would so plainly be anything but slow, insensitive, and unimaginative. He would not be tied to the heavy lorry-wheels of the realist, but would soar over the Tower Bridge on wings; and we should say sadly to ourselves, 'If only bargees were really like that!'

And in a little while they would become more like that.

– The End of a Chapter –

I have been asked by an Editor to explain how it comes about that he has printed the last Christopher Robin story. In these cases it is generally the Editor who offers an apologetic explanation to the author; and though I am proud that it is not so now, I feel a little diffident about putting what is really a personal matter before a probably uninterested public. However, one can't go on defying an Editor . . . so here goes.

To begin at the beginning: When Christopher Robin was born, he had to have a name. We had already decided to call him something else, and later on he decided to call himself something still else, so that the two names for which we were now looking were to be no more than an excuse for giving him two initials for use in later life. I had decided on two initials rather than one or none, because I wanted him to play cricket for England, like W. G. Grace and C. B. Fry, and if he was to play as an amateur, two initials would give him a more hopeful appearance on the score-card. A father has to think of these things. So, one of us liking the name Christopher, and the other maintaining that Robin was both pleasing and unusual, we decided that as C. R. Milne he should be encouraged to make his name in the sporting world.

'Christopher Robin', then, he became on some legal document, but as nobody ever called him so, we did not think any more about it. However, three years later I wrote a book called *When We Were Very Young*, and since he was much in my mind when I wrote it, I dedicated it to him. Now there is something about this book which I must explain; namely, that the adventures of a child as therein put down came from three sources.

1. My memories of my own childhood.

2. My imaginings of childhood in general.

3. My observations of the particular childhood with which I was now in contact.

As a child I kept a mouse; probably it escaped − they generally do. Christopher Robin has kept almost everything except a mouse. As a child I played lines-and-squares in a casual sort of way. Christopher Robin never did until he read what I had written about it, and not very enthusiastically then. But he did go to Buckingham Palace a good deal (which I didn't), though not with Alice. And most children hop . . . and sometimes they sit half-way down the stairs − or, anyway, I can imagine them doing so . . . and Christopher Robin was very proud of his first pair of braces, though I never heard that he wanted a tail particularly . . . And so on, and so on.

Well, now, you will have noticed that the words 'Christopher Robin' come very trippingly off the tongue. I noticed that too. You simply can't sit down to write verses for children, in a house with a child called (however officially only) Christopher Robin, without noticing it.

> Christopher Robin goes
> Hoppity hoppity –

Practically it writes itself.
But now consider:

> Christopher Robin had
> Great big
> Waterproof
> Boots on . . .

Hopeless. It simply must be John.

So it happened that into some of the verses the name Christopher Robin crept, and into some it didn't; and if you go through the book carefully, you will find that Christopher Robin is definitely associated with – how many do you think? – only three sets of verses. Three out of forty-four!

You can imagine my amazement and disgust, then, when I discovered that in a night, so to speak, I had been pushed into a back place, and that the hero of *When We Were Very Young* was not, as I had modestly expected, the author, but a curiously-named child of whom, at this time, I had scarcely heard. It was this Christopher Robin who kept mice, walked on the lines and not in the squares, and wondered what to do on a spring morning; it was this Christopher Robin, not I, whom Americans were clamouring to see; and, in fact (to make due acknowledgement at last), it was this Christopher Robin, not I, not the publishers, who was selling the book in such large and ridiculous quantities.

Now who was this Christopher Robin – the hero now, since it was so accepted, of *When We Were Very Young;* soon to be the hero of *Winnie-the-Pooh* and two other books? To me he was, and remained, the child of my imagination. When I thought of him, I thought of him in the Forest, living in his tree as no child really lives; not in the nursery, where a differently-named child (so far as we in this house are concerned) was playing with his animals. For this reason I have not felt self-conscious when writing about him, nor apologetic at the thought of exposing my own family to the public gaze. The 'animals', Pooh and Piglet, Eeyore, Kanga, and the rest, are in a different case. I have not 'created' them. He and his mother gave them life, and I have just 'put them into a book'. You can see them now in the nursery, as Ernest Shepard saw them before he drew them. Between us, it may be, we have given them shape, but you have only to look at them to see, as I saw at once, that Pooh is a Bear of Very Little Brain, Tigger Bouncy, Eeyore Melancholy and so on. I have exploited them for my own profit, as I feel I have not exploited the legal Christopher Robin. All I have got from Christopher Robin is a name which he never uses, an introduction to his friends . . . and a gleam which I have tried to follow.

However, the distinction, if clear to me, is not so clear to others; and to them, anyhow, perhaps to me also, the dividing line between the imaginary and the legal Christopher Robin becomes fainter with each book. This, then, brings me (at last) to one of the reasons why these verses and stories have come to an end. I feel that the legal Christopher Robin has already had more publicity than I want for him. Moreover, since he is growing up, he will soon feel that he has had more publicity than he wants for himself. We all, young and old, hope to make some sort of a name, but we want to make it in our own chosen way, and, if possible, by our own exertions. To be the hero of the '3 not out' in that heroic finish between Oxford and Cambridge (Under Ten), to be undisputed Fluff Weight Champion (four stone six) of the Lower School, even to be the only boy of his age who can do Long Division: any of these is worth much more than all your vicarious literary reputations. Lawrence hid himself in the Air Force under the name of Shaw to avoid being introduced for the rest of his life as 'Lawrence of Arabia'. I do not want C. R. Milne ever to wish that his names were Charles Robert.

Now for the second reason; for I would not have you think that I am a model of unselfishness and parental duty, who never comes to a decision save in the interests of another. No doubt you who read this will remember the occasion when you first met Mr Snooks, the famous author, at a party. He had just published *Woodlice.* You smiled graciously upon him, you said a few nice things about his books . . . and you came away with the feeling that Snooks was the most rude, intolerable and boorish fellow you had ever met. 'My dear,' you said to your friend, 'I simply *fawned* on the man, and he looked as if he wanted to *bite* me!'

Well, that often happens. But authors are not really so vain and so self-conscious as you think. Your fault was not in praising Snooks too little or too much, but in praising him for the wrong thing. If you told Snooks that you adored *Slugs,* I am not surprised that he scowled at you. If you committed the unforgivable sin, and said to him, 'Why don't you write some more books like *Centipedes*?' – then I am not surprised that he looked like biting you. The wonder is that he didn't actually do it. I certainly should have. But if you had praised *Woodlice,* he must have trembled with inarticulate gratitude.

For all an author's hopes and fears and interests are centred in his latest book. As he writes 'The End', he is saying to himself, 'The best thing I have done.' In his heart he may know it is not the best, but he longs to think it is, and will love you for helping him to persuade himself.

Can I go on writing these books, and persuade myself that each is better than the one before? I don't see how it is possible. Darwin, or somebody, compared the world of knowledge to a circle of light. The bigger the circumference of light, the bigger the surrounding border of darkness waiting to be lit up. A child's world of the imagination is not like that. As children we have explored it from end to end, and the map of it lies buried somewhere in our hearts, drawn in symbols whose meaning we have forgotten. A gleam from outside may light it up for us, so that for a moment it becomes clear again, and in that precious moment we can make a copy of it for others. But when the light has gone, to go on making fair copies of that copy – is it worth it?

For writing, let us confess it unashamed, is fun. There are those who will tell you that it is an inspiration, they sing but as the linnet sings; there are others, in revolt against such priggishness, who will tell you that it is simply a business like any other. Others, again, will assure you (heroically) that it is an agony, and they would sooner break stones – as well they might. But though there is something of inspiration in it, something of business, something, at times, of agony, yet, in the main, writing is just thrill; the thrill of exploring. The more difficult the country, the more untraversed by the writer, the greater (to me, anyhow) the thrill.

Well, I have had my thrill out of children's books, and know that I shall never recapture it. At least, not until I am a grandfather.

MARRIED LIFE

– Wedding Bells –

C hampagne is often pleasant at lunch, it is always delightful at dinner, and it is an absolute necessity, if one is to talk freely about oneself afterwards, at a dance supper. But champagne for tea is horrible. Perhaps this is why a wedding always finds me melancholy next morning. 'She has married the wrong man,' I say to myself. 'I wonder if it is too late to tell her.'

The trouble of answering the invitation and of thinking of something to give more original than a toast rack should, one feels, have its compensations. From each wedding that I attend I expect an afternoon's enjoyment in return for my egg stand. For one thing I have my best clothes on. Few people have seen me in them (and these few won't believe it), so that from the very beginning the day has a certain freshness. It is not an ordinary day. It starts with this advantage, that in my best clothes I am not difficult to please. The world smiles upon me.

Once I am in church, however, my calm begins to leave me. As time wears on, and the organist invents more and more tunes, I tremble lest the bride has forgotten the day. The choir is waiting for her; the bridegroom is waiting for her. I – I also – wait. What if she has changed her mind at the last minute? But no. The organist has sailed into his set piece; the choir advances; follows the bride looking so lonely that I long to comfort her and remind her of my egg stand; and, last of all, the pretty bridesmaids. The clergyman begins his drone.

You would think that, reassured by the presence of the bride, I could be happy now. But there is still much to bother me. The bridegroom is showing signs of having forgotten his part, the bride can't get her glove off, one of the bridesmaids is treading on my hat. Worse than all this, there is a painful want of unanimity among the congregation as to when we stand up and when we sit down. Sometimes I am alone and sitting when everybody else is standing, and that is easy to bear; but sometimes I find myself standing when everybody else is sitting, and that is very hard.

They have gone to the vestry. The choir sings an anthem to while away the kissing-time, and, right or wrong, I am sitting down, comforting my poor hat. There was a time when I, too, used to go into the vestry; when I was something of an authority on weddings, and would attend weekly in some minor official capacity. Any odd jobs that were going seemed to devolve on me. If somebody was wanted suddenly to sign the register, or kiss the bride's mother, or wind up the going-away car, it used to be taken for granted that I was the man to do it. I wore a white flower in my button-hole to show that I was available. I served, I may say, in an entirely honorary capacity, except in so far as I was expected to give the happy pair a slightly larger present than the others. One day I happened to suggest to an intending groom that he had other friends more ornamental, and therefore more suitable for this sort of work, than I; to which he replied that they were all married, and that etiquette demanded a bachelor for the business. Of course, as soon as I heard this I got married too.

Here they come. 'Doesn't she look sweet?' We hurry after them and rush for the carriages. I am only a friend of the bridegroom's; perhaps I had better walk.

It must be very easy to be a guest at a wedding reception, where each of the two clans takes it for granted that all the extraordinary strangers belong to the other clan. Indeed, nobody with one good suit, and a stomach for champagne and sandwiches, need starve in London. He or she can wander safely in wherever a red carpet beckons. I suppose I must put in an appearance at this reception, but if I happen to pass another piece of carpet on the way to the house, and the people going in seem more attractive than our lot, I shall be tempted to join them.

This is, perhaps, the worst part of the ceremony, this three hundred yards or so from the hymn-sheets to the champagne. All London is now gazing at my old top-hat. When the war went on and on and on, and it seemed as though it were going on for ever, I looked back on peace much as those old retired warriors at the end of last century looked back on their happy Crimean days; and in the same spirit as that in which they hung their swords over the baronial fire-place, I decided to suspend my old top-hat above the mantelpiece in the drawing-room. In the years to come I would take my grandchildren on my knee and tell them stories of the old days when grandfather was a civilian, of desperate charges by church-wardens and organists, and warm receptions; and sometimes I would hold the old top-hat reverently in my hands, and a sudden gleam would come into my eyes, so that those watching me would say to each other, 'He is thinking of that tea-fight at Rutland Gate in 1912'. So I pictured the future for my top-hat, never dreaming that in 1920 it would take the air again.

For I went into the war in order to make the world safe for democracy, which I understood to mean (and was distinctly informed so by the press) a world safe for those of us who prefer soft hats with a dent in the middle. 'The war,' said the press, 'has killed the top-hat.' Apparently it failed to do this, as it failed to do so many of the things which we hoped from it. So the old veteran of 1912 dares the sunlight again.

We are arrived, and I am greeted warmly by the bride's parents. I look at the mother closely so that I shall know her again when I come to say good-bye, and give her a smile which tells her that I was determined to come down to this wedding although I had a good deal of work to do. I linger with the idea of pursuing this point, for I want them to know that they nearly missed me, but I am pushed on by the crowd behind me. The bride and bridegroom salute me cordially but show no desire for intimate gossip. A horrible feeling goes through me that my absence would not have been commented upon by them at any inordinate length. It would not have spoilt the honeymoon, for instance.

I move on and look at the presents. The presents are numerous and costly. Having discovered my own I stand a little way back and listen to the opinions of my neighbours upon it. On the whole the reception is favourable. The detective, I am horrified to discover, is on the other side of the room, apparently callous as to the fate of my egg stand. I cannot help feeling that if he knew his business he would be standing where I am standing now; or else there should be two detectives. It is a question now whether it is safe for me to leave my post and search for food . . . Now he is coming round; I can trust it to him.

On my way to the refreshments I have met an old friend. I like to meet my friends at weddings, but I wish I had not met this one. She has sowed the seeds of disquiet in my mind by telling me that it is not etiquette to begin to eat until the bride has cut the cake. I answer, 'Then why doesn't somebody tell the bride to cut the cake?' but the bride, it seems, is busy. I wish now that I had not met my friend. Who but a woman would know the etiquette of these things, and who but a woman would bother about it?

The bride is cutting the cake. The bridegroom has

lent her his sword, or his fountain-pen, whatever is the emblem of his trade – he is a stock-broker – and as she cuts, we buzz round her, hoping for one of the marzipan pieces. I wish to leave now, before I am sorry, but my friend tells me that it is not etiquette to leave until the bride and bridegroom have gone. Besides, I must drink the bride's health. I drink her health; hers, not mine.

Time rolls on. I was wrong to have had champagne. It doesn't suit me at tea. However, for the moment life is bright enough. I have looked at the presents and my own is still there. And I have been given a bagful of confetti. The weary weeks one lives through without a handful of anything to throw at anybody. How good to be young again. I take up a strong position in the hall.

They come . . . Got him – got him! Now a long shot – got him! I feel slightly better, and begin the search for my hostess . . .

I have shaken hands with all the bride's aunts and all the bridegroom's aunts, and in fact all the aunts of everybody here. Each one seems to me more like my hostess than the last. 'Good-bye!' Fool – of course – there she is. 'Good-bye!'

My hat and I take the air again. A pleasant afternoon; and yet to-morrow morning I shall see things more clearly, and I shall know that the bridegroom has married the wrong girl. But it will be too late then to save him.

– Love and Marriage –

I s love necessary to a happy married life? It depends on what you mean by 'love'. My answer to the question would be that what I mean by 'love' is only experienced by the happily married. Obviously I do not mean 'married' in the technical sense. No formula of Church or State makes two people one. But it is not until a man and woman have lived together for years in utter contentment of each other that they know what love is; as distinct from passion, as distinct from affection, as distinct from friendliness, community of interest, good-comradeship; as distinct from everything else which this world has to offer. Is love necessary to a happy married life? Well, then, it depends on what you mean by 'happy'.

Married life, of course, is difficult. It would hardly offer such complete happiness if it were not. The Victorians found it more easy. The wife said 'Yes, John' and 'No, John', and went on having children. Was the husband happy? At least he was comfortable; and part of his comfort was derived from the fact that his marriage was a success. Never a disagreement between them! 'Yes, John,' 'No, John.' Was the wife happy? I know of Victorian women who spent the first five years of their married lives in an agony of fear: fear that they were going to have children, fear of the children whom they knew they were going to have. No doubt the husband had often said at the club, cigar in mouth, 'My wife has no secrets from me.' Yet I think she had this one secret. Otherwise, surely, he could not have been so comfortable.

Today women have no secrets from us. It makes life more difficult. That is why we dislike beggars in the street; not because they pester us, but because we are reminded of their shameful secret; their poverty. How easy marriage would be if we could go on saying '*My* house', '*my* children', '*my* money', and the woman went on saying 'Yes, John', and kept her secrets to herself; just as the fox keeps his secret to himself, and enables us to assure him that he enjoys being hunted. But Woman talks to us now as man to man, and Man is suddenly in the horrible position of realizing that 'a happy marriage' in some ridiculous way has got to mean happiness for the woman also. Is it any wonder that there is this rush of unhappy marriages? What would happen to all the happy shooting-parties each autumn, if they had suddenly to include happiness for a vocal pheasant?

But are we, then, to renounce the real happy marriage as too difficult of attainment? Those who are content with what is called the 'French marriage' have already done so. If marriage in France is truly regarded as a means to one end only, the founding of a family, no doubt a 'safe' marriage – in which little of value, as between husband and wife, is given, and little asked – is the best form of marriage possible. But I confess (and I am aware that it may be a personal idiosyncrasy of mine) that mere propagation has never seemed to me an overwhelming achievement in itself. To provide the next generation seems to me less praiseworthy than to provide *for* the next generation, and even this is less important than that the present generation should do something of value with its own lives. One really happy marriage today is a greater achievement than the provision of human material for a thousand loveless marriages in the future. To miss the most beautiful thing in life in order that there shall be a next generation to miss it too, is a poor way of expressing one's personality. Not for a moment do I deny that there is beauty in childhood, beauty in motherhood, beauty in the relation of parent to child. If any man or woman says 'I love children; I have not the temperament for a happy marriage, but I could make a child happy. And I want to experience the joys of fatherhood or motherhood,' then let him or her make a 'safe' marriage, convenient for the purpose. But if he says, 'I must marry so as to keep up the birthrate,' then honestly I do not know what he is talking about. Is he trying to help God – or the British Empire? Probably he makes no distinction.

How can the happy marriage be achieved? I think it is less a matter of choice and more a matter of temperament than is supposed. The assumption of every unhappy husband is that if he had only met Mary before he met Jane, all would have been well, and that, as soon as Jane has divorced him, he and Mary will at last have a chance of being happy together. I fancy that it is a small chance. He didn't choose the wrong woman; he was, and will always be, the wrong man. I shall never win the Mixed Doubles at Wimbledon, however carefully I choose my partner. My form is hopeless for Wimbledon anyhow. There are thousands of men and women whose form is hopeless for Dunmow.

What, then, is the correct form? I should say it was found in an eagerness, all day and every day, to see things from the point of view of the other. It is difficult; particularly for the man, who can never quite forget that his wife promised to obey him . . . and never quite remember that he has endowed her with all his goods. It is always difficult to see the other person's point of view; always lamentably easy to say 'Oh, but that's different.' However, one gets better with practice.

And is this, you ask, what I mean by love – just seeing things from each other's point of view, making allowances for each other? Of course not. This is merely the top-dressing which gives the ache, the longing, the glory, the misery, all that you first felt when you pledged yourselves to each other, a chance to grow into real love. Love, as I mean it, can only be experienced by the happily married, but I doubt if the happily married will ever experience it unless they were 'in love' at some time first. So perhaps that is the answer to the question.

– The Order of the Bath –

'We must really do something about the bath,' said Celia.

'We must,' I agreed.

At present what we do is this. Punctually at six-thirty or nine, or whenever it is, Celia goes in to make herself clean and beautiful for the new day, while I amuse myself with a razor. After a quarter of an hour or so she gives a whistle to imply that the bathroom is now vacant, and I give another one to indicate that I have only cut myself once. I then go hopefully in and find that the bath is half full of water; whereupon I go back to my room and engage in Dr Hugh de Sélincourt's physical exercises for the middle-aged. After these are over I take another look, at the bath, discover that it is now three-eights full, and return to my room and busy myself with Dr Archibald Marshall's mental drill for busy men. By the time I have committed three Odes of Horace to memory, it may be low tide or it may not; if not, I sit on the edge of the bath with the daily paper and read about the latest strike – my mind occupied equally with wondering when the water is going out and when the brick-layers are. And the thought that Celia is now in the dining-room eating more than her share of the toast does not console me in the least.

'Yes,' I said, 'it's absurd to go on like this. You had better see about it today, Celia.'

'I don't think – I mean, I think – you know, it's really *your* turn to do something for the bathroom.'

'What do you mean, *my* turn? Didn't I buy the glass shelves for it? You'd never even heard of glass shelves.'

'Well, who put them up after they'd been lying about for a month?' said Celia. 'I did.'

'And who bumped his head against them the next day? I did.'

'Yes, but that wasn't really a *useful* thing to do. It's your turn to be useful.'

'Celia, this is mutiny. All household matters are supposed to be looked after by you. I do the brain work; I earn the money; I cannot be bothered with these little domestic worries. I have said so before.'

'I sort of thought you had.'

You know, I am afraid that is true.

'After all,' she went on, 'the drinks are in your department.'

'Hock, perhaps,' I said; 'soapy water, no. There is a difference.'

'Not very much,' said Celia.

By the end of another week I was getting seriously alarmed. I began to fear that unless I watched it very carefully I should be improving myself too much.

'While the water was running out this morning,' I said to Celia, as I started my breakfast just about lunch-time, 'I got *Paradise Lost* off by heart, and made five hundred and ninety-six revolutions with the back paws. And then it was time to shave myself again. What a life for a busy man!'

'I don't know if you know that it's no – '

'Begin again,' I said.

' – that it's no good waiting for the last inch or two to go out by itself. Because it won't. You have to – to *hoosh* it out.'

'I do. And I sit on the taps looking like a full moon and try to draw it out. But it's no good. We had a neap tide today and I had to hoosh four inches. Jolly.'

Celia gave a sigh of resignation.

'All right,' she said, 'I'll go to the plumber today.'

'Not the plumber,' I begged. 'On the contrary. The plumber is the man who *stops* the leaks. What we really want is an unplumber.'

We fell into silence again.

'But how silly we are!' cried Celia suddenly. 'Of course!'

'What's the matter now?'

'The bath is the *landlord's* business! Write and tell him.'

'But – but what shall I say?' Somehow I knew Celia would put it on to me.

'Why, just – *say*. When you're paying the rent, you know.'

'I – I see.'

I retired to the library and thought it out. I hate

writing business letters. The result is a mixture of formality and chattiness which seems to me all wrong.

My first letter to the landlord went like this:

DEAR SIR, — I enclose cheque in payment of last quarter's rent. Our bath won't run out properly. Yours faithfully.

It is difficult to say just what is wrong with that letter, and yet it is obvious that something has happened to it. It isn't *right*. I tried again.

DEAR SIR, – Enclosed please find cheque in payment of enclosed account. I must ask you either to enlarge the exit to our bath or to supply an emergency door. At present my morning and evening baths are in serious danger of clashing. Yours faithfully.

My third attempt had more sting in it:

DEAR SIR, — Unless you do something to our bath I cannot send you enclosed cheque in payment of enclosed account. Otherwise I would have. Yours faithfully.

At this point I whistled to Celia and laid the letters before her.

'You see what it is,' I said. 'I'm not quite getting the note.'

'But you're so abrupt,' she said. 'You must remember that this is all coming quite as a surprise to him. You want to lead up to it more gradually.'

'Ah, perhaps you're right. Let's try again.'

I tried again, with this result:

DEAR SIR, – In sending you a cheque in payment of last quarter's rent I feel I must tell you how comfortable we are here. The only inconvenience – and it is indeed a trifling one, dear Sir – which we have experienced is in connexion with the bathroom. Elegantly appointed and spacious as this room is, commodious as we find the actual bath itself, yet we feel that in the matter of the waste-pipe the high standard of efficiency so discernible elsewhere is sadly lacking. Were I alone I should not complain; but unfortunately there are two of us; and, for the second one, the weariness of waiting while the waters of the first bath exude drop by drop is almost more than can be borne. I speak with knowledge, for it is I who –

I tore the letter up and turned to Celia.

'I'm a fool,' I said. 'I've just thought of something which will save me all this rotten business every morning.'

'I'm so glad. What is it?'

'Why, of course – in future *I* will go to the bath first.'

And I do. It is a ridiculously simple solution and I cannot think why it never occurred to me before.

– Heavy Work –

E very now and then doctors slap me about and ask me if I was always as thin as this.

'As thin as what?' I say with as much dignity as is possible to a man who has had his shirt taken away from him.

'As thin as this,' says the doctor, hooking his stethoscope on to one of my ribs, and then going round to the other side to see how I am getting on there.

I am slightly better on the other side, but he runs his pencil up and down me and produces that pleasing noise which small boys get by dragging a stick along railings.

I explain that I was always delicately slender, but that latterly my ribs have been overdoing it.

'You must put on more flesh,' he says sternly, running his pencil up and down them again. (He must have been a great nuisance as a small boy.)

'I will,' I say fervently, 'I will.'

Satisfied by my promise he gives me back my shirt.

But it is not only the doctor who complains; Celia is even more upset by it. She says tearfully that I remind her of a herring. Unfortunately she does not like herrings. It is my hope some day to remind her of a turbot and make her happy. She, too, has my promise that I will put on flesh.

We had a fortnight's leave a little while ago, which seemed to give me a good opportunity of putting some on. So we retired to a house in the country where there is a weighing-machine in the bathroom. We felt that the mere sight of this weighing-machine twice daily would stimulate the gaps between my ribs. They would realize that they had been brought down there on business.

The first morning I weighed myself just before stepping into the water. When I got down to breakfast I told Celia the result.

'You *are* a herring,' she said sadly.

'But think what an opportunity it gives me. If I started the right weight, the rest of the fortnight would be practically wasted. By the way, the doctor talks about putting on flesh, but he didn't say how much he wanted. What do you think would be a nice amount?'

'About another stone,' said Celia. 'You were just a nice size before the War.'

'All right. Perhaps I had better tell the weighing-machine. This is a co-operative job; I can't do it all myself.'

The next morning I was the same as before, and the next, and the next, and the next.

'Really,' said Celia, pathetically, 'we might just as well have gone to a house where there wasn't a weighing-machine at all. I don't believe it's trying. Are you sure you stand on it long enough?'

'Long enough for me. It's a bit cold, you know.'

'Well, make quite sure to-morrow. I must have you not quite so herringy.'

I made quite sure the next morning. I had eight stone and a half on the weight part, and the-little-thing-you-move-up-and-down was on the '4' notch, and the bar balanced midway between the top and the bottom. To have had a crowd in to see would have been quite unnecessary; the whole machine was shouting eight-stone-eleven as loudly as it could.

'I expect it's got used to you,' said Celia when I told her the sad state of affairs. 'It likes eight-stone-eleven people.'

'We will give it', I said, 'one more chance.'

Next morning the weights were as I had left them, and I stepped on without much hope, expecting that the bar would come slowly up to its midway position of rest. To my immense delight, however, it never hesitated but went straight up to the top. At last I had put on flesh!

Very delicately I moved the-thing-you-move-up-and-down on to its next notch. Still the bar stayed at the top. I had put on at least another ounce of flesh!

I continued to put on more ounces. Still the bar remained up! I was eight-stone-thirteen . . . Good heavens, I was eight-stone-fourteen!

I pushed the-thing-you-move-up-and-down back to the zero position, and exchanged the half-stone weight for a stone one. Excited but a trifle cold, for it was a fresh morning, and the upper part of the window was wide open, I went up from nine stone ounce by ounce . . .

At nine-stone-twelve I jumped off for a moment and shut the window . . .

At eleven-stone-eight I had to get off again in order to attend to the bath, which was in danger of overflowing . . .

At fifteen-stone-eleven the breakfast gong went . . . At nineteen-stone-nine I realized that I had overdone it. However I decided to know the worst. The worst that the machine could tell me was twenty-stone-seven. At twenty-stone-seven I left it.

Celia, who had nearly finished breakfast, looked up eagerly as I came in.

'Well?' she said.

'I am sorry I am late,' I apologized, 'but I have been putting on flesh.'

'Have you really gone up?' she asked excitedly.

'Yes.' I began mechanically to help myself to porridge, and then stopped. 'No, perhaps not,' I said thoughtfully. 'Have you gone up much?'

'Much,' I said. 'Quite much.'

'How much? Quick!'

'Celia,' I said sadly, 'I am twenty-stone-seven. I may be more; the weighing-machine gave out then.'

'Oh, but, darling, that's much too much.'

'Still, it's what we came here for,' I pointed out. 'No, no bacon, thanks; a small piece of dry toast.'

'I suppose the machine couldn't have made a mistake?'

'It seemed very decided about it. It didn't hesitate at all.'

'Just try again after breakfast to make sure.'

'Perhaps I'd better try now,' I said, getting up, 'because if I turned out to be only twenty-stone-six I might venture on a little porridge after all. I shan't be long.'

I went upstairs. I didn't dare face that weighing-machine in my clothes after the way in which I had already strained it without them. I took them off hurriedly and stepped on. To my joy the bar stayed in its downward position. I took off an ounce . . . then another ounce. The bar remained down . . .

At eighteen-stone-two I jumped off for a moment in order to shut the window, which some careless housemaid had opened again . . .

At twelve-stone-seven I shouted through the door to Celia that I shouldn't be long, and that I should want the porridge after all . . .

At four-stone-six I said that I had better have an egg or two as well.

At three ounces I stepped off, feeling rather shaken.

I have not used the weighing-machine since; partly because I do not believe it is trustworthy, partly because I spent the rest of my leave in bed with a severe cold. We are now in London again, where I am putting on flesh. At least the doctor who slapped me about yesterday said that I must, and I promised him that I would.

HOME LIFE

– Fixtures and Fittings –

T here was once a young man who decided to be a poodle-clipper. He felt that he had a natural bent for it, and he had been told that a fashionable poodle-clipper could charge his own price for his services. But his father urged him to seek another profession. 'It is an uncertain life, poodle-clipping,' he said. 'To begin with, very few people keep poodles at all. Of these few, only a small proportion wants its poodles clipped. And, of this small proportion, a still smaller proportion is likely to want its poodles clipped by *you*.' So the young man decided to be a hair-dresser instead.

I thought of this story the other day when I was bargaining with a house-agent about 'fixtures', and I decided that no son of mine should become a curtain-pole manufacturer. I suppose that the price of a curtain-rod (pole or perch) is only a few shillings, and, once made, it remains in a house for ever. Tenants come and go, new landlords buy and sell, but the old brass rod stays firm at the top of the window, supporting curtain after curtain. How many new sets are made in a year? No more, it would seem, than the number of new houses built. Far better, then, to manufacture an individual possession like a toothbrush, which has the additional advantage of wearing out every few months.

But from the consumer's point of view, a curtain-rod is a pleasant thing. He has the satisfaction of feeling that, having once bought it, he has bought it for the rest of his life. He may change his house and with it his fixtures, but there is no loss on the brass part of the transaction, however much there may be on the bricks and mortar. What he pays out with one hand, he takes in with the other. Nor is his property subject to the ordinary mischances of life. There was an historic character who 'lost the big drum,' but he would become even more historic who had lost a curtain-rod, and neither parlour-maid nor cat is ever likely to wear a guilty conscience over the breaking of one.

I have not yet discovered, in spite of my recent familiarity with house-agents, the difference between a fixture and a fitting. It is possible that neither word has any virtue without the other, as is the case with 'spick' and 'span', One has to be both; however dapper, one would never be described as a span gentleman. In the same way it may be that a curtain-rod or an electric light is never just a fixture or a fitting, but always 'included in the fixtures and fittings'. Then there is a distinction, apparently, between a 'landlord's fixture' and a 'tenant's fixture', which is rather subtle. A fire-dog is a landlord's fixture; so is a door-plate. If you buy a house you get the fire-dogs and the door-plates thrown in, which seems unnecessarily generous. I can understand the landlord deciding to throw in the walls and the roof, because he couldn't do much with them if you refused to take them, but it is a mystery why he should include a door-plate, which can easily be removed and sold to somebody else. And if a door-plate, why not a curtain-rod? A curtain-rod is a necessity to the incoming tenant; a door-plate is merely a luxury for the grubby-fingered to help them to keep the paint clean. One might be expected to bring one's own door-plate with one, according to the size of one's hand.

For the whole idea of a fixture or fitting can only be that it is something about which there can be no individual taste. We furnish a house according to our own private fancy; the 'fixtures' are the furnishings in regard to which we are prepared to accept the general fancy. The other man's curtain-rod, though easily detachable and able to fit a hundred other windows, is a fixture; his carpet-as-planned (to use the delightful language of the house-agent), though securely nailed down and the wrong size for any other room but this, is not a fixture. Upon some such reasoning the first authorized schedule of fixtures and fittings must have been made out.

It seems a pity that it has not been extended. There are other things than curtain-rods and electric-light bulbs which might be left behind in the old house and picked up again in the new. The silver cigarette-box, which we have all had as a birthday or wedding present, might safely be handed over to the incoming tenant, in the certainty that another just like it will be waiting for us in our next house. True, it will have different initials on it, but that will only make it the more interesting, our own having become fatiguing to us by this time. Possibly this sort of thing has already been done in an unofficial way among neighbours. By mutual agreement they leave their aspidistras and their 'Maiden's Prayer' behind them. It saves trouble and expense in the moving, which is an important thing in these days, and there would always be the hope that the next aspidistra might be on the eve of flowering or laying eggs, or whatever it is that its owner expects from it.

– The Cupboard –

I t was the landlord who first called my attention to the cupboard; I should never have noticed it myself.

'A very useful cupboard you see there,' he said; 'I should include that in the fixtures.'

'Indeed,' said I, not at all surprised; for the idea of his taking away the cupboard had not occurred to me.

'You won't find many rooms in London with a cupboard like that.'

'I suppose not,' I said. 'Well, I'll let you have my decision in a few days. The rent with the cupboard, you say, is – ' And I named the price.

'Yes, with the cupboard.'

So that settled the cupboard question.

Settled it so far as it concerned him. For me it was only the beginning. In the year that followed my eyes were opened, so that I learned at last to put the right value on a cupboard. I appreciate now the power of the mind which conceived this thing, the nobility of the great heart which included it among the fixtures. And I am not ungrateful.

You may tell a newly married man by the way he talks of his garden. The pretence is that he grows things there – verbenas and hymantifilums and cinerarias, anything which sounds; but of course one knows that what he really uses it for is to bury in it things which he doesn't want. Some day I shall have a garden of my own in which to conduct funerals with the best of them; until that day I content myself with my cupboard.

It is marvellous how things lie about and accumulate. Until they are safely in the cupboard we are never quite at ease; they have so much to say outside, and they put themselves just where you want to step, and sometimes they fall on you. Yet even when I have them in the cupboard I am not without moments of regret. For later on I have to open it to introduce companions, and then the sight of some old friend saddens me with the thought of what might have been. 'Oh, and I did mean to hang you up over the writing-desk,' I say remorsefully.

I am thinking now of a certain picture – a large portrait, of my old head-master. It lay in a corner for months, waiting to be framed, getting more dingy and dirty every day. For the first few weeks I said to myself, 'I must clean that before I send it to the shop. A piece of bread will do it.' Later, 'It's extraordinary how clever these picture people are. You'd think it was hopeless now, but I've no doubt, when I take it round to-morrow –'

A month after that somebody trod on it . . .

Now, then, I ask you – what could I do with it but put it in the cupboard? You cannot give a large photograph of a head-master, bent across the waistcoat, to a housekeeper, and tell her that you have finished with

it. Nor would a dustman make it his business to collect pedagogues along with the usual cabbage stalks. A
married man would have buried it under the begonia;
but having no garden . . .

That is my difficulty. For a bachelor in chambers
who cannot bury, there should be some other consum-
ing element than fire. In the winter I might possibly
have burnt it in small quantities – Monday the head,
Tuesday the watch-chain – but in the summer what
does one do with it? And what does one do with the
thousands of other things which have had their day –
the old magazines, letters, papers, collars, chair-legs,
broken cups? You may say that, with the co-operation
of my housekeeper, a firmer line could be adopted
towards some of them. Perhaps so; but, alas! she is a
willing accessory to my weakness. I fancy that once, a
long time ago, she must have thrown away a priceless
MS. in an old waistcoat; now she takes no risks with
either. In principle it is a virtue; in practice I think I
would chance it.

It is a big cupboard; you wouldn't find many
rooms in London with a cupboard like that; and it is
included in the fixtures. Yet in the ordinary way, I suppose, I could not go on putting things in for ever. One
day, however, I discovered that a family of mice had
heard of it too. At first I was horrified. Then I saw that
it was all for the best; they might help me to get rid
of things. In a week they had eaten three pages of a
nautical almanac; interesting pages which would be of

real help to a married man at sea who wished to find the latitude by means of two fixed stars, but which, to a bachelor on the fourth floor, were valueless.

The housekeeper missed the point. She went so far as to buy me an extremely patient mouse-trap. It was a silly trap, because none of the mice knew how to work it, although I baited it once with a cold poached egg. It is not for us to say what our humbler brethren should like and dislike; we can only discover by trial and error. It occurred to me that, if they *did* like cold poached eggs, I should be able to keep on good terms with them, for I generally had one over of a morning. However, it turned out that they preferred a vegetable diet – almanacs and such . . .

The cupboard is nearly full. I don't usually open it to visitors, but perhaps you would care to look inside for a moment?

That was once a top-hat. What do *you* do with your old top-hats? Ah, yes, but then I only have a housekeeper here at present . . . That is a really good pair of boots, only it's too small . . . All that paper over there ? Manuscript . . . Well, you see it *might* be valuable one day . . .

Broken batting glove. Brown paper – I always keep brown paper, it's useful if you're sending off a parcel. *Daily Mail* war map. Paint-pot – doesn't belong to me really, but it was left behind, and I got tired of kicking it over. Old letters – all the same handwriting, bills probably . . .

Ah, no, they are not bills, you mustn't look at those. (I didn't know they were there – I swear I didn't. I thought I had burnt them.) Of course I see now that she was quite right. ... Yes, that was the very sweet one where she . . . well, I knew even then that . . . I mean I'm not complaining at all, we had a very jolly time . . .

Still, if it *had* been a little different – if that last letter . . . Well, I might by now have had a garden of my own in which to have buried all this rubbish.

– The Stream –

At the end of the meadow into which our garden wanders is a stream. This is called The River. Between the garden and the meadow is a ditch. This is called The Brook. In front of the house the brook has been widened between sandstone walls into a piece of water forty yards long by four across, and this piece of water is called The Stream. Now we know where we are.

When we came here, the stream had no containing walls, but followed an irregular course over the unlevelled ground, so that here and there little islands showed themselves above the water, and on these islands water-rats would polish up their whiskers. It was all very rural, and sometimes I wish that we had left it like that. But when the brook dried up in summer, making the stream all island, one felt that somehow a reserve of water must be kept in being. Could we collect enough in a deepened, widened and walled-in stream to last us through a drought? The question was never answered, for it was at this moment that I discovered The Spring.

I forget who discovered the source of the Nile, but probably he felt much as I did when I scratched a way of escape for the puddles on the sloping lawn which fell to the stream, and found an hour later that the puddles were still full. This end of the little lawn had been a rubbish-heap when we came. We had cleared away the rubbish, and filled in the ground, but it had remained boggy and unpleasant. Now we knew why. So we dug out an irregular pool (The Spring) eight feet in diameter and four feet deep, lined it with sandstone, ringed it with limestone, dotted it with that stuff which looks like rhubarb but isn't, and gave it a channel into the stream; and, ever since, water has flowed down this channel at the rate of a thousand gallons a day.

To the simple-minded a thousand anything sounds a lot, and perhaps they are now picturing to themselves a foaming cascade leaping and tumbling on its way to the stream. Actually this does not happen. The over-flow (as the arithmetical may discover) fills a glass in a little less than six seconds, which means that it is a pleasant, fair-sounding trickle. But the trickle goes on for ever. And though the brook does not conform to this literary tradition, feeling perhaps (and quite rightly) that what it would do for Tennyson, it certainly won't do for me, yet it does help to feed the stream all through the winter; sometimes, indeed, to repletion; and even in the summer it renews its activity after every rainstorm. In short, the stream may properly be described as running water; and at the east end, running out through a narrow opening in what must be called (still using these grandiloquent terms) The Stone Bridge, it becomes the brook again.

Into this stream we put a few goldfish. They made themselves at home in the weeds and reeds and mud, and we saw less of them than we had hoped. But they were not idle. Raking out the weeds one day, I found that I had brought up some little black-and-silver sparklets, which looked more like metallic fish than real ones. Gossip-writers tell us of well-known people who breed Corgis or Siamese cats; and though one suspects that it is the Corgis or the cats who do most of the work, one assumes that the so-called breeders are not taken by surprise. We were. I can think of no surprise more delightful than the discovery that a rake-full of weed taken from a rapidly congesting stream is alive with little silver fish. Of all Nature's bounties this seems for the moment the most bountiful. Suddenly the whole Universe becomes a possibility.

By the summer we had hundreds of goldfish in the stream, and on hot afternoons they lay about in glittering pools of light like a Turner sunset reflected in still water. We had other fish, not always identified, which came 'out of the everywhere' in that mysterious way only to be explained by Nature's abhorrence of a vacuum. Here was some not wholly occupied water, why not fill it? So she filled it with little fish and tritons and newts and water-beetles and everything else she could think of at the time, including grass-snakes.

One does not take kindly at first to grass-snakes. The big four-footers look horribly menacing in the water, as indeed, they are to the gentler inhabitants, and the babies, slow-worm size, are even more unlovable. I hoicked a big one out with a putter at our first acquaintance, and having knocked it on the head before it could collect itself and ask 'Where am I?' I went away to collect the family – my own family, I mean. When we came back, it lay there dead, with, by its side, a disgorged and elongated frog stretched out to nearly a foot in length. I felt sorry then for having killed it (and sorry, of course, for the frog), and have taken no action against grass-snakes since, save to hoick an occasional one out of the water – a sport little practised, but demanding a delicacy of approach, and an exact calculation of the centre of gravity of the quarry, unrivalled in other sports.

With all these fish in the water, the heron and the kingfisher have come and been welcome, earning their keep by the beauty they have brought. A pair of mallards have nested in the reeds; and once a swan found here a home from home. During a trial flight from a lake a few miles away it had developed engine trouble, and crash-landed in our little lane. We carried it down to the stream, and there it stayed for a few days, coming out occasionally to visit us through the open doors of the sitting-room. Having regained its nerve, and had a practice flight or two, it rejoined its family. But each year swallows play follow-my-leader down the length of the stream, touch and away; dragon-flies of every colour and size dart from point to point, and hover like helicopters; and from his home in the bank a water-rat launches himself silently, leaving no trace.

The strangest visitor to the stream was a stoat. I was in a deck-chair on the lawn, when it came from the rhododendron bushes on the opposite side of the stream, in search, it seemed, of a water-rat. Diving eagerly into the first hole it saw, it popped out, before it was quite ready, at the water end. Its enthusiasm slightly damped, it scrambled to land, shook itself, and went into the next hole. Once more a startled face shot into the stream; once more a dripping but still business-like back was climbing out. At the third hole, surely, somebody would be in. Nobody was. There was a third splash. And now, just opposite to me, it stood upright on its back legs, fingering its chin, and thinking back to the day when its mother had first told it about water-rats. Something had slipped up. For a minute it stood there, wondering how it had got the thing wrong; per-haps it was rabbits, not water-rats; perhaps – and then, with a final shake, which seemed equally a bodily and mental dispersion of all this water, it dropped on to its fore-legs and stole back into the bushes.

So, one way and another, we have had great delight from our stream. But nothing lasts in a garden. There came a winter when the river rose to the top of its ten-foot banks and raced over the meadow; the stream merged into the general flood; and the rose-garden became a swimming-pool. Our goldfish left us and were last heard of at Sheerness. Then, on the day after the drive down from the lane had been re-surfaced with whatever chemical material was called for, the rains came, and poisoned water poured down the hill, and in the morning most of the natural inhabitants of the stream were dying or dead. Finally, the spring developed an oily orange scum, due to the iron in the water, and from being our pride was now our shame; so that we had to fill it in and cover it up, leaving only its outlet into the stream. But now the stream at that end became oilier, and scummier, and, because we had lost interest, more overgrown with weeds. Slowly the weeds and the scum moved towards the bridge, and even the water-rats deserted the banks, even the frogs came no longer to spawn. Well, we have had our fun from the stream. Nothing lasts in a garden, nothing stays the same. But something else takes its place. Perhaps one day it will be an orangery.

– Cotchford Farm –

The farmhouse wherein we live is a very old one. None can say exactly how old; but because it is still marked as a farm in the ordnance map, so it is still known. It had been more or less derelict for some years before we came. The lovely old house could be made habitable, and a barn turned into a garage with rooms for a gardener above it, but most of the outbuildings were as forlorn as Mariana; and as they gradually fell to pieces we used the wood and the bricks for other purposes, and let such fields to a neighbouring farmer as we were not going to make into a garden. For ourselves we have bred no more than goldfish and fattened no more than a few pigs.

One day during the war, having to be in London for various reasons, I went into a large store to buy a sponge. We pumped our own water at that time, so we could not complain of its quality, but it was death to sponges. All the springs in these parts have iron in them, and the iron enters into the soul of the sponge, making the yellow, as Macbeth was saying, one red; after which the whole thing disintegrates.

The price of a sponge has always come as something of a shock to me. Sponges don't look expensive, as does a charmingly coloured piece of soap embossed

Rêve d'Amour. They have a ragged, uncared-for appearance, as if their owner had never taken any pride in them. One feels that one should get for one's money something more regular in shape, with fewer holes in it. It is true that sponges live at the bottom of the sea, which makes the overhead considerable, but there seems to be no lack of them. The love-life of a sponge is not a subject on which one can ponder for long without becoming unsettled; enough to know that in course of time, and after some pretty confusion by the bride when hinting at the possibility, they have small sponges. And so the breed goes on. A static life, I have often thought, being a sponge; but, of course, an absorbing one.

I chose a large, healthy specimen, once, no doubt, the pride of the reef. Its price was wired on to it; otherwise I should have supposed the figure to be a rough valuation of the department, or possibly the whole store. When I had made the necessary calculations, 'this way and that dividing the swift mind' – banker, solicitor, stockbroker – I gave the assistant my name and address.

The girl's face lit up. This does happen sometimes, and on the rare occasions when it does, my face lights up too. It was pleasant to think that she had read my books, or (more probably) knew somebody who had. We smiled at each other in a friendly way, and she said that I must be feeling proud of myself. I gave a modest imitation of a man who prefers to have it said rather than to say it.

'Taking a holiday now?' she asked.

This puzzled me a little. One need not take a long holiday in order to buy a sponge; and, of course, if one had known the price, one would have known that one couldn't afford to. There was no reason why I shouldn't have left my heroine in my hero's arms, dashed to London, bought sponge, and dashed back in time to hear her say: 'Oh, darling, I never dreamed it would be like this!' However, I gave her another smile, and went to another department to buy a pair of slippers.

It was to a man this time that I gave my name. His face also lit up; so, of course, did mine. Never before had I been such a public character. He said:

'Well, you've been doing a fine bit of work.'

Had I known him better, I should have asked him to which manifesto or pamphlet he was referring, for one likes to be told these things. As it was, I said with a shrug: 'Oh well, we must all do what we can.'

He agreed.

'Got it all in?' he went on.

This baffled me. It seemed to be, but could hardly be, a low reference to the nominal fee which I accept sometimes for these things. But, before I could answer, he added – and so put the afternoon at last in its true perspective:

'We owe a lot to you farmers.'

After all these years of authorship it is disheartening to find that it is not one's name but one's address which raises admiration in the breasts of strangers. Yet if one is to be mistaken for what one is not, I would as soon be thought a farmer as anything. I was to make a speech once at a City dinner, and the stranger next to my wife, having consulted her name-card and the menu, said:

'I see your husband is talking to us tonight. Let me see, isn't he something to do with the Gas, Light and Coke Company?'

That, I think, did me an injustice; the other did not. Indeed I have sometimes played with the idea of making this place a farm again, but the amount of writing which it would involve has stayed me. I do enough writing anyway.

At the beginning of the war the Army wanted to requisition a piece of waste land for which we had never found a use. I made no objection, and was sent a form to fill up, so that a fair rental might be fixed. I had to answer about sixty questions: the acreage of the land, how long I had owned it, what I had paid for it, what crops I had grown on it; its value as grassland if I hadn't ploughed it up, its value as ploughland if I didn't use it for grazing; my rotation of crops for the last six years; the average profit I should expect from turnips, from swedes, from oats, from raspberries, from chickens, from curly-kale; my outgoings on artificial manures – there were spaces for all these things and many more.

I just couldn't think of the answers. All it grew, besides bracken and bramble, was cowslips. After sleepless days and nights and many false beginnings, I wrote diagonally across the form: 'I give you the thing.' I had a most charming letter of thanks in return; I didn't know that Government departments could be so grateful.

PUBLIC LIFE

– In London –

I was very fond of London; so fond of it, in fact, that I liked it for what it was and not for what it might have been. When I was a boy, or perhaps a little earlier, whiskered young men called Edwin used to assure bashful young women called Angelina that they were the most divine and peerless angels in the world, without fault or blemish; and if Angelina suggested modestly from beneath drooping eyelashes that sometimes she feared that her temper was a little short (or her nose a little long), Edwin would protest passionately that indeed no, his darling was utterly, utterly perfect. This is one sort of love. Cowper, less deeply enamoured, was inspired to say, 'England, with all thy faults I love thee still', which was very handsome of him, though it was no way to talk to a lady. However, no doubt he felt like that even about Mrs Unwin. But the true lover neither maintains that the loved one is faultless, nor feels the need to explain that he loves her in spite of her faults. He recognizes the faults as themselves objects of affection. With a more beautiful nose Angelina would not be Angelina. It is her absurd nose which makes her so much more lovable than Cleopatra. And that is just how I have always felt about London.

The test question for the lover of London is to be found on the Surrey side of the river. Before there was any talk of Festivals, did you want to improve the Surrey side or didn't you? If all those old wharves and warehouses were pulled down – or, in the case of the wharves, pulled up – if all the wharves and warehouses were destroyed, and a nice new Embankment were built like the nice fairly new Embankment on the north side of the river, then we should have an Embankment on each side of the Thames in London, just as they have an Embankment on each side of the Seine in Paris. Wouldn't that be nice?

For myself I cannot understand the passion for making things, places, people like something or somebody else. The only lasting virtue is individuality. The charm of London to a lover of London is that it is not in the least like Paris; just as the charm of Paris to a Parisian is that it is not in the least like London. It is true that of this and that we may say that they order these things better in France, but let us go to France and watch them doing it . . . and then come back to London. Don't ask me to tell you why I love the King's Road (there is only one King's Road: down which Charles II travelled to call upon his Nell in Chelsea); travel down it yourself from Eaton Square to World's End, and tell yourself that of all the unlovely roads . . . well, but think how many mothers love unlovely sons, and wouldn't change them for the most beautiful film star. Silly, but that is how we get to feel.

I am afraid that I have been carried away, as I always am when I think of the vandals who would improve London into something which was not London, and spoil my river for me. For the London which I meant to write about was not a collection of bricks and stone, nor a smudge on an atlas, but a state of being. A man who confessed that he was living in Sin might give the impression that he was some sort of an Anglo-Indian, just as a woman living in Holy Wedlock could be visualized as tucked away in Shropshire. It sounds much the same whether you live in Luxor or Luxury, and a Yorkshireman could undoubtedly live in something like Idleness. Living in London has an equally deceptive sound at first hearing. 'So that's where he lives,' you say to yourself, when you should be saying 'So that's how he lives.'

The charm of London which remains, however often other people have written about it, is that one can live there as an individual and not as one of a community. I suppose that one is born with or without the communal feeling, and that to be born without it is to be uncivic, unpatriotic, selfish, and totally unworthy to be (as I rather think I am) Vice-President of the local Horticultural Society. Am I uncivic? Very well, then, I am uncivic. I can love a place without loving all the people in it; I can be proud of what its heroes have done without wanting to kiss them. (As they do in France, by the way.) For nothing can make me want to know people, just because they are handy. If I do meet them, I am as capable of liking them as anybody else, but I don't go about thinking, 'Oh, if only I could meet somebody!' as people with the communal sense seem to do. I prefer to choose my friends because I like them, not because they are neighbours; and if this means often enough that they don't choose me because they don't like me, well, how right they are.

In all the years when I lived in a flat I never knew the man below. It is true that I continually corresponded with him in (on my part) dignified and courtly phrases, beginning 'Dear Sir' and ending 'Yours faithfully', and explaining in between just why my bath-water came through his ceiling – a simple mathematical explanation, invoking the Law of Archimedes and the Law of Gravity, which I need not bother you with now. But I never spoke to him; and if I did meet him on the stairs or in the street, it was not to recognize him as the gentleman who was getting his head wet. In all the years during which I lived in a London house I never knew my neighbours on either side. On one occasion, in the household's absence, a burglar visited us and withdrew with a bagful of loot. One of our neighbours, suspecting after ten years' proximity that this was not the lawful owner coming out, followed behind in some vague hope of giving evidence if a policeman intervened, or of picking up the bag if it were accidentally dropped. Whatever his intentions, he gave me written information of the burglary (which, indeed, had already proclaimed itself), and of the fact that he had so nearly arrested the intruder. Naturally I wrote and thanked him. But I still didn't know what he looked like.

Well, that was my London. I liked the look of it and the feel of it and the blessed independence of it. I also liked much of the entertainment which it offered. And since I would rather read the news than have it read aloud to me, I liked being able to go round the corner for a Late Night Final. I didn't know the paper-man's name, nor he mine, but we smiled at each other in a friendly way. I liked that too. I like to be free to smile at the person who serves me, without struggling to remember whether the baby is a boy or a girl, whether lettuces or rheumatism should be the object of my congratulation or concern. In short, I am damnably uncivic.

– The Painter –

Mr Paul Samways was in a mood of deep depression. The artistic temperament is peculiarly subject to these moods, but in Paul's case there was reason why he should take a gloomy view of things. His masterpiece, 'The Shot Tower from Battersea Bridge', together with the companion picture, 'Battersea Bridge from the Shot Tower', had been purchased by a dealer for seventeen and sixpence. His sepia monochrome, 'Night,' had brought him an IOU for five shillings. These were his sole earnings for the last six weeks, and starvation stared him in the face.

'If only I had a little capital!' he cried aloud in despair, 'Enough to support me until my Academy picture is finished.' His Academy picture was a masterly study entitled, 'Roll on, thou deep and dark blue ocean, roll,' and he had been compelled to stop halfway across the Channel through sheer lack of ultramarine.

The clock struck two, reminding him that he had not lunched. He rose wearily and went to the little cupboard which served as a larder. There was but little there to make a satisfying meal – half a loaf of bread, a corner of cheese, and a small tube of Chinese-white. Mechanically he set the things out . . .

He had finished, and was clearing away, when there came a knock at the door. His charwoman, whose duty it was to clean his brushes every week, came in with a card.

'A lady to see you, sir,' she said.

Paul read the card in astonishment.

'The Duchess of Winchester,' he exclaimed. 'What on earth. Show her in, please.' Hastily picking up a brush and the first tube which came to hand, he placed himself in a dramatic position before his easel and set to work.

'How do you do, Mr Samways?' said the Duchess.

'G – good afternoon,' said Paul, embarrassed both by the presence of a duchess in his studio and by his sudden discovery that he was touching up a sunset with a tube of carbolic tooth-paste.

'Our mutual friend, Lord Ernest Topwood, recommended me to come to you.'

Paul, who had never met Lord Ernest, but had once seen his name in a ha'penny paper beneath a photograph of Mr Arnold Bennett, bowed silently.

'As you probably guess, I want you to paint my daughter's portrait.'

Paul opened his mouth to say that he was only a landscape painter, and then closed it again. After all, it was hardly fair to bother her Grace with technicalities.

'I hope you can undertake this commission,' she said, pleadingly.

'I shall be delighted,' said Paul. 'I am rather busy

just now, but I could begin at two o'clock on Monday.'
'Excellent!' said the Duchess. 'Till Monday, then.' And
Paul, still clutching the toothpaste, conducted her to
her carriage.

Punctually at three-fifteen on Monday Lady
Hermione appeared. Paul drew a deep breath of astonishment when he saw her, for she was lovely beyond
compare. All his skill as a landscape painter would
be needed if he were to do justice to her beauty. As
quickly as possible he placed her in position and set
to work.

'May I let my face go for a moment?' said Lady
Hermione after three hours of it.

'Yes, let us stop,' said Paul. He had outlined her in
charcoal and burnt cork, and it would be too dark to
do any more that evening.

'Tell me where you first met Lord Ernest?' she
asked as she came down to the fire.

'At the Savoy, in June,' said Paul boldly.

Lady Hermione laughed merrily. Paul, who had
not regarded his last remark as one of his best things,
looked at her in surprise.

'But your portrait of him was in the Academy in
May!' she smiled.

Paul made up his mind quickly.

'Lady Hermione,' he said with gravity, 'do not
speak to me of Lord Ernest again. 'Nor', he added
hurriedly, 'to Lord Ernest of me. When your picture
is finished I will tell you why. Now it is time you went.'

He woke the Duchess up, and made a few common-place remarks about the weather. 'Remember,' he whispered to Lady Hermione as he saw them to their car. She nodded and smiled.

The sittings went on daily. Sometimes Paul would paint rapidly with great sweeps of the brush; sometimes he would spend an hour trying to get on his palette the exact shade of green bice for the famous Winchester emeralds, sometimes in despair he would take a sponge and wipe the whole picture out, and then start madly again. And sometimes he would stop work altogether and tell Lady Hermione about his home-life in Worcestershire. But always, when he woke the Duchess up at the end of the sitting, he would say, 'Remember!' and Lady Hermione would nod back at him.

It was a spring-like day in March when the picture was finished, and nothing remained to do but to paint in the signature.

'It is beautiful!' said Lady Hermione with enthusiasm, 'Beautiful! Is it at all like me?'

Paul looked from her to the picture, and back to her again.

'No,' he said, 'not a bit. You know, I am really a landscape painter.'

'What do you mean?' she cried. 'You are Peter Samways, A.R.A., the famous portrait painter!'

'No,' he said sadly. 'That was my secret. I am Paul Samways. A member of the Amateur Rowing Association, it is true, but only an unknown landscape painter.

Peter Samways lives in the next studio, and he is not even a relation.'

'Then you have deceived me! You have brought me here under false pretences!' She stamped her foot angrily, 'My father will not buy that picture, and I forbid you to exhibit it as a portrait of myself.'

'My dear Lady Hermione,' said Paul, 'you need not be alarmed. I propose to exhibit the picture as "When the Heart is Young". Nobody will recognize a likeness to you in it. And if the Duke does not buy it, I have no doubt that some other purchaser will come along.'

Lady Hermione looked at him thoughtfully. 'Why did you do it?' she asked gently.

'Because I fell in love with you.'

She dropped her eyes, and then raised them gaily to his. 'Mother is still asleep,' she whispered.

'Hermione!' he cried, dropping his palette and putting his brush behind his ear.

She held out her arms to him.

As everybody remembers, 'When the Heart is Young,' by Paul Samways, was the feature of the Exhibition. It was bought for £10,000 by a retired bottle manufacturer, whom it reminded a little of his late mother. Paul woke to find himself famous. But the success which began for him from this day did not spoil his simple and generous nature. He never forgot his brother artists, whose feet were not yet on the top of the ladder. Indeed, one of his first acts after he was married was to give a commission to Peter Samways, A.R.A. – nothing less than the painting of his wife's portrait. And Lady Hermione was delighted with the result.

– The Younger Son –

I t is a hard thing to be the younger son of an ancient but impoverished family. The fact that your brother Thomas is taking most of the dibs restricts your inheritance to a paltry two thousand a year, while pride of blood forbids you to supplement this by following any of the common professions. Impossible for a St Verax to be a doctor, a policeman, or an architect. He must find some nobler means of existence.

For three years Roger St Verax had lived precariously by betting. To be a St Verax was always to be a sportsman. Roger's father had created a record in the sporting world by winning the Derby and the Waterloo Cup with the same animal – though, in each case, it narrowly escaped disqualification. Roger himself almost created another record by making betting pay. His book, showing how to do it, was actually in the press when disaster overtook him.

He began by dropping (in sporting parlance) a cool thousand on the Jack Joel Selling Plate at Newmarket. On the next race he dropped a cool five hundred, and later on in the afternoon a cool seventy-five pounds ten. The following day found him at Lingfield, where *he* dropped a cool monkey (to persevere with the language of the racing stable) on the Solly Joel

Cup, picked it up on the next race, dropped a cool pony, dropped another cool monkey, dropped a cool wallaby, picked up a cool hippopotamus, and finally, in the last race of the day, dropped a couple of lukewarm ferrets. In short, he was (as they say at Tattersall's Corner) entirely cleaned out.

When a younger son is cleaned out there is only one thing for him to do. Roger St Verax knew instinctively what it was. He bought a new silk hat and a short black coat, and went into the City.

What a wonderful place, dear reader, is the City! You, madam, who read this in your daintily uphol-stered boudoir, can know but little of the great heart of the City, even though you have driven through its arteries on your way to Liverpool Street Station, and have noted the bare and smoothly brushed polls of the younger natives. You, sir, in your country vicarage, are no less innocent, even though on sultry afternoons you have covered your head with the Financial Supple-ment of *The Times* in mistake for the Literary Supple-ment, and have thus had thrust upon you the stirring news that Bango-Bangos were going up. And I, dear friends, am equally ignorant of the secrets of the Stock Exchange. I know that its members frequently walk to Brighton, and still more frequently stay there; that while finding a home for all the good stories which have been going the rounds for years, they sometimes invent entirely new ones for themselves about the Chancellor of the Exchequer; and that they sing the

National anthem very sternly in unison when occasion demands it. But there must be something more in it than this, or why are Bango-Bangos still going up?

I don't know. And I am sorry to say that even Roger St Verax, a Director of the Bango-Bango Development Company, is not very clear about it all.

It was as a Director of the Bango-Bango Exploration Company that he took up his life in the City. As its name implies, the Company was originally formed to explore Bango-Bango, an impenetrable district in North Australia; but when it came to the point it was found much more profitable to explore Hampstead, Clapham Common, Blackheath, Ealing, and other rich and fashionable suburbs, A number of hopeful ladies and gentlemen having been located in these parts, the Company went ahead rapidly, and in 1907 a new prospector was sent out to replace the one who was assumed to have been eaten.

In 1908 Roger first heard the magic word 'reconstruction', and to his surprise found himself in possession of twenty thousand pounds and a Directorship of the new Bango-Bango Mining Company.

In 1909 a piece of real gold was identified, and the shares went up like a rocket.

In 1910 the Stock Exchange suddenly woke to the fact that rubber tyres were made of rubber, and in a moment the Great Boom was sprung upon an amazed City. The Bango-Bango Development Company was immediately formed to take over the Bango-Bango

Mining Company (together with its prospector, if alive, its plants, shafts and other property, not forgetting the piece of gold), and more particularly to develop the vegetable resources of the district with a view to planting rubber trees in the immediate future. A neatly compiled prospectus put matters very clearly before the stay-at-home Englishman. It explained quite concisely that, supposing the trees were planted so many feet apart throughout the whole property of five thousand square miles, and allowing a certain period for the growth of a tree to maturity, and putting the average yield of rubber per tree at, in round figures, so much, and assuming for the sake of convenience that rubber would remain at its present price, and estimating the cost of working the plantation at say, roughly, £100,000, why, then it was obvious that the profits would be anything you liked up to two billion a year – while (this was important) more land could doubtless be acquired if the shareholders thought fit. And even if you were certain that a rubber tree couldn't possibly grow in the Bango-Bango district (as in confidence it couldn't), still it was worth taking shares purely as an investment, seeing how rapidly rubber was going up; not to mention the fact that Roger St Verax, the well-known financier, was a Director . . . and so on.

In short, the Bango-Bango Development Company was, in the language of the City, a safe thing.

Let me hasten to the end of this story. At the end

of 1910 Roger was a millionaire; and for quite a week afterwards he used to wonder where all the money had come from. In the old days, when he won a cool thousand by betting, he knew that somebody else had lost a cool thousand by betting, but it did not seem to be so in this case. He had met hundreds of men who had made fortunes through rubber; he had met hundreds who bitterly regretted that they had missed making a fortune; but he had never met any one who had lost a fortune. This made him think the City an even more wonderful place than before.

But before he could be happy there remained one thing for him to do: he must find somebody to share his happiness. He called on his old friend, Mary Brown, one Sunday.

'Mary,' he said, with the brisk confidence of the City man, 'I find I'm disengaged next Tuesday. Will you meet me at St George's Church at two? I should like to show you the curate and the vestry, and one or two things like that.'

'Why, what's happened?'

'I am a millionaire,' said Roger calmly. 'So long as I only had my beggarly pittance, I could not ask you to marry me. There was nothing for it but to wait in patience. It has been a long, weary wait, dear, but the sun has broken through the clouds at last. I am now in a position to support a wife. Tuesday at two,' he went on, consulting his pocket diary; 'or I could give you half an hour on Monday morning.'

'But why this extraordinary hurry? Why mayn't I be married properly, with presents and things.'

'My dear,' said Roger reproachfully, 'you forget. I am a City man now, and it is imperative that I should be married at once. Only a married man, with everything in his wife's name can face with confidence the give and take of the bustling City.'

MEDITATIVE LIFE

– By the Sea –

I t is very pleasant in August to recline in Fleet Street, or wherever stern business keeps one, and to think of the sea. I do not envy the millions at Margate and Blackpool, at Salcombe and Minehead, for I have persuaded myself that the sea is not what it was in my day. Then the pools were always full of starfish; crabs – really big crabs – stalked the deserted sands; and anemones waved their feelers at you from every rock.

Poets have talked of the unchanging sea (and they may be right as regards the actual water), but I fancy that the beach must be deteriorating. In the last ten years I don't suppose I have seen more than five starfishes, though I have walked often enough by the margin of the waves – and not only to look for lost golf balls. There have been occasional belated little crabs whom I have interrupted as they were scuttling home, but none of those dangerous monsters to whom in fearful excitement, and as a challenge to one's companion, one used to offer a forefinger. I refuse regretfully your explanation that it is my finger which is bigger; I should like to think that it were indeed so, and that the boys and girls of today find their crabs and starfishes in the size and quantity to which I was accustomed. But I am afraid we cannot hide it from ourselves that the supply is giving out. It is in fact obvious that one cannot keep on taking starfishes home and hanging them up in the hall as barometers without detriment to the coming race.

We had another amusement as children, in which I suppose the modern child is no longer able to indulge. We used to wait until the tide was just beginning to go down, and then start to climb round the foot of the cliffs from one sandy bay to another. The waves lapped the cliffs, a single false step would have plunged us into the sea, and we had all the excitement of being caught by the tide without any of the danger. We had the further excitement, if we were lucky, of seeing frantic people waving to us from the top of the cliff, people of inconceivable ignorance, who thought that the tide was coming up and that we were in desperate peril. But it was a very special day when that happened.

I have done a little serious climbing since those days, but not any which was more enjoyable. The sea was never more than a foot below us and never more than two feet deep, but the shock of falling into it would have been momentarily as great as that of falling down a precipice. You had therefore the two joys of climbing – the physical pleasure of the accomplished effort, and the glorious mental reaction when your heart returns from the middle of your throat to its normal place in your chest. And you had the additional advantages that you couldn't get killed, and that, if an insuperable difficulty presented itself, you were not driven back, but merely waited five minutes for the tide to lower itself and disclose a fresh foothold.

But, as I say, these are not joys for the modern child. The tide, I dare say, is not what it was – it does not, perhaps, go down so certainly. Or the cliffs are of a different and of an inferior shape. Or people are no longer so ignorant as *to* mistake the nature of your position. One way or another I expect I do better in Fleet Street. I shall stay and imagine myself by the sea; I shall not disappoint myself with the reality.

But I imagine myself away from hands and piers; for a band by a moonlit sea calls you to be very grown-up, and the beach and the crabs – such as are left – call you to be a child; and between the two you can very easily be miserable. I can see myself with a spade and bucket being extraordinarily happy. The other day I met a lucky little boy who had a pile of sand in his garden to play with, and I was fortunate enough to get an order for a tunnel. The tunnel which I constructed for him was a good one, but not so good that I couldn't see myself building a better one with practice. I came away with an ambition for architecture. If ever I go to the sea again I shall build a proper tunnel; and afterwards – well, we shall see. At the moment I feel in tremendous form. I feel that I could do a cathedral.

There is one joy of childhood, however, which one can never recapture, and that is the joy of getting wet in the sea. There is a statue not so far from Fleet Street of the man who introduced Sunday schools into England, but the man whom boys and girls would really like to commemorate in lasting stone is the doctor who first said that salt water couldn't give you a cold. Whether this was true or not I do not know, but it was a splendid and never-failing retort to anxious grown-ups, and added much to the joys of the seaside. But it is a joy no longer possible to one who is his own master. I, for instance, can get my feet wet in fresh water if I like; to get them wet in salt water is no special privilege.

Feeling as I do, writing as I have written, it is sad for me to know that if I really went to the sea this August it would not be with a spade and a bucket but with a bag of golf clubs; that even my evenings would be spent, not on the beach, but on a bicycle riding to the nearest town for a paper. Yet it is useless for you to say that I do not love the sea with my old love, that I am no longer pleased with the old childish things. I shall maintain that it is the sea which is not what it was, and that I am very happy in Fleet Street thinking of it as it used to be.

– Midsummer Day –

There is magic in the woods on Midsummer Day – so people tell me. Titania conducts her revels. Let others attend her court; for myself I will beg to be excused. I have no heart for revelling on Midsummer Day. On any other festival I will be as jocund as you please, but on the longest day of the year I am over-burdened by the thought that from this moment the evenings are beginning to draw in. We are on the way to winter.

It is on Midsummer Day, or thereabouts, that the cuckoo changes his tune, knowing well that the best days are over and that in a little while it will be time for him to fly away. I should like this to be a learned article on 'The Habits of the Cuckoo', and yet, if it were, I doubt if I should love him at the end of it. It is best to know only the one thing of him, that he lays his eggs in another bird's nest – a friendly idea – and beyond that to take him as we find him. And we find that his only habit which matters is the delightful one of saying 'Cuckoo'.

The nightingale is the bird of melancholy, the thrush sings a disturbing song of the good times to come, the blackbird whistles a fine, cool note which goes best with a February morning, and the skylark trills his way to a heaven far out of the reach of men; and what the lesser white-throat says I have never rightly understood. But the cuckoo is the bird of present joys; he keeps us company on the lawns of summer, he sings under a summer sun in a wonderful new world of blue and green. I think only happy people hear him. He is always about when one is doing pleasant things. He never sings when the sun hides behind banks of clouds, or if he does, it is softly to himself so that he may not lose the note. Then 'Cuckoo!' he says aloud, and you may be sure that everything is warm and bright again.

But now he is leaving us. Where he goes I know not, but I think of him vaguely as at Mozambique, a paradise for all good birds who like their days long. If geography were properly taught at schools, I should know where Mozambique was, and what sort of people live there. But it may be that, with all these cuckoos cuckooing and swallows swallowing from July to April, the country is so full of immigrants that there is no room for a stable population. It may also be, of course, that Mozambique is not the place I am thinking of; yet it has a birdish sound.

The year is arranged badly. If Mr Willett were alive he would do something about it. Why should the days begin to get shorter at the moment when summer is fully arrived? Why should it be possible for the vicar to say that the evenings are drawing in, when one is still having strawberries for tea? Sometimes I think that if June were called August, and April June, these things would be easier to bear. The fact that in what is now called August we should be telling each other how wonderfully hot it was for October would help us to bear the slow approach of winter. On a Midsummer Day in such a calendar one would revel gladly, and there would be no midsummer madness.

Already the oak trees have taken on an autumn look. I am told that this is due to a local irruption of caterpillars, and not to the waning of the summer, but it has a suspicious air. Probably the caterpillars knew. It seems strange now to reflect that there was a time when I liked caterpillars; when I chased them up sub-urban streets, and took them home to fondle them; when I knew them all by their pretty names, assisted them to become chrysalises, and watched over them in that unprotected state as if I had been their mother. Ah, how dear were my little charges to me then! But now I class them with mosquitoes and blight and har-vesters, the pests of the countryside. Why, I would let them crawl up my arm in those happy days of old, and now I cannot even endure to have them dropping gently into my hair. And I should not know what to say to a chrysalis.

There are great and good people who know all about solstices and zeniths, and they can tell you just why it is that 24th June is so much hotter and longer than 24th December – why it is so in England, I should say. For I believe (and they will correct me if I am wrong) that at the equator the days and nights are always of equal length. This must make calling almost an impossibility, for if one cannot say to one's hostess, 'How quickly the days are lengthening (or drawing in),' one might as well remain at home. 'How stationary the days are remaining' might pass on a first visit, but the old inhabitants would not like it rubbed into them. They feel, I am sure, that however saddening a Midsummer Day may be, an unchanging year is much more intolerable. One can imagine the superiority of a resident who lived a couple of miles off the equator, and took her visitors proudly to the end of the garden where the seasons were most mutable. There would be no bearing with her.

In these circumstances I refuse to be depressed. I console myself with the thought that if 25th June is the beginning of winter, at least there is a next summer to which I may look forward. Next summer anything may happen. I suppose a scientist would be considerably surprised if the sun refused to get up one morning, or, having got up, declined to go to bed again. It would not surprise me. The amazing thing is that Nature goes on doing the same things in the same way year after year; any sudden little irrelevance on her part would be quite understandable. When the wise men tell us so confidently that there will be an eclipse of the sun in 1921, invisible at Greenwich, do they have no qualms of doubt as the day draws near? Do they glance up from their whitebait at the appointed hour, just in case it is visible after all? Or if they have journeyed to Pernambuco, or wherever the best view is to be obtained, do they wonder whether . . . perhaps . . . and tell each other the night, before that, of course, they were coming to Pernambuco anyhow, to see an aunt?

Perhaps they don't. But for myself I am not so certain, and I have hopes that, certainly next year, possibly even this year, the days will go on lengthening after midsummer is over.

– Geographical Research –

T he other day I met a man who didn't know where Tripoli was. Tripoli happened to come into the conversation, and he was evidently at a loss. 'Let's see,' he said. 'Tripoli is just down by the – er – you know. What's the name of that place?' 'That's right,' I answered, 'just opposite Thingumabob. I could show you in a minute on the map. It's near – what do they call it?' At this moment the train stopped, and I got out and went straight home to look at my atlas.

Of course I really knew exactly where Tripoli was. About thirty years ago, when I learnt geography, one of the questions they were always asking me was, 'What are the exports of Spain, and where is Tripoli?' But much may happen in twenty years; coast erosion and tidal waves and things like that. I looked at the map in order to assure myself that Tripoli had remained pretty firm. As far as I could make out it had moved. Certainly it must have looked different thirty years ago, for I took some little time to locate it. But no doubt one's point of view changes with the decades. To a boy Tripoli might seem a long way from Italy – even in Asia Minor; but when he grew up his standards of measurement would be altered.

Tripoli would appear in its proper place due south of Sicily.

I always enjoy these periodic excursions to my atlas. People talk a good deal of nonsense about the importance of teaching geography at school instead of useless subjects like Latin and Greek, but so long as you have an atlas near you, of what use is geography? Why waste time learning where Tripoli and Fiume are, when you can turn to a map of Africa and spot them in a moment? In a leading article in *The Times* (no less – our premier English newspaper) it was stated during a general election that Darlington was in Yorkshire. You may say that *The Times* leader writers ought to have been taught geography; I say that unfortunately they *have* been taught geography. They learnt, or thought they learnt, that Darlington was a Yorkshire town. If they had been left in a state of decent ignorance, they would have looked for Darlington in the map and found that it was in Durham. (One moment – Map 29 – Yes, Durham; that's right.) As it is, there are at this moment some hundreds of retired colonels who go about believing implicitly that Darlington is in Yorkshire because *The Times* has said it. How much more important than a knowledge of geography is the possession of an atlas.

My own atlas is a particularly fine specimen. It contains all sorts of surprising maps which never come into ordinary geography. I think my favourite is a picture of the Pacific Ocean, coloured in varying shades of blue according to the depths of the sea. The deep ultramarine terrifies me. I tremble for a ship which is passing over it, and only breathe again when it reaches the very palest blue. There is one little patch – the Nero Deep in the Ladrone Basin – which is actually 31,614 ft. deep. I suppose if you sailed over it you would find it no bluer than the rest of the sea, and if you fell into it you would feel no more alarmed than if it were 31,613 ft. deep; but still you cannot see it in the atlas without a moment's awe.

Then my atlas has a map of 'The British Empire showing the great commercial highways'; another of 'The North Polar regions showing the progress of explorations'; maps of the trade routes, of gulf streams, and beautiful things of that kind. It tells you how far it is from Southampton to Fremantle, so that if you are interested in the M.C.C. Australian team you can follow them day by day across the sea. Why, with all your geographical knowledge you couldn't even tell me the distance between Yokohama and Honolulu, but I can give the answer in a moment – 3,379 miles. Also I know exactly what a section of the world along lat. 45 deg. N. looks like – and there are very few of our most learned men who can say as much.

But my atlas goes even farther than this, though I for one do not follow it. It gives diagrams of exports and imports; it tells you where things are manufactured or where grown; it gives pictures of sheep – an immense sheep representing New Zealand and a mere insect representing Russia, and alas! no sheep at all for Canada and Germany and China. Then there are large cigars for America and small mild cigars for France and Germany; pictures in colour of such unfamiliar objects as spindles and raw silk and miners and Mongolians and iron ore; statistics of traffic receipts and diamonds. I say that I don't follow my atlas here, because information of this sort does not seem to belong properly to an atlas. This is not my idea of geography at all. When I open my atlas I open it to look at maps – to find out where Tripoli is – not to acquire information, about flax and things; yet I cannot forego the boast that if I wanted I could even speak at length about flax.

And lastly there is the index. Running my eye down it, I can tell you in less than a minute where such different places as Jorobado, Kabba, Hidegkut, Paloo, and Pago Pago are to be found. Could you, even after your first-class honours in the Geography Tripos, be as certain as I am? Of Hidegkut, perhaps, or Jorobado, but not of Pago Pago.

On the other hand, you might possibly have known where Tripoli was.

– The Mathematical Mind –

M y daily paper just now is full of mathematical difficulties, submitted by its readers for the amusement of one of its staff. Every morning he appeals to us for assistance in solving tricky little problems about pints of water and herrings and rectangular fields. The magic number '9' has a great fascination for him. It is terrifying to think that if you multiply any row of figures by 9 the *sum* of the figures thus obtained is divisible by 9. It is uncanny to hear that if a clock takes six seconds to strike six it takes as much as thirteen seconds and a fifth to strike twelve.

As a relief from searching for news in a press devoid of news, the study of these problems is welcome enough, and to the unmathematical mind, no doubt, the solutions appear to be something miraculous. But to the mathematical mind a thing more miraculous is the awe with which the unmathematical regard the simplest manipulation of figures. Most of my life at school was spent in such pursuits that I feel bound to claim the mathematical mind to some extent, with the result that I can look down wonderingly upon these deeps of ignorance yawning daily in the papers – much, I dare say, as the senior wrangler looks down upon me. Figures may puzzle me occasionally, but at least they never cause me surprise or alarm.

Naturally, then, I am jealous for the mathematical mind. If a man who makes a false quantity, or attributes Lycidas to Keats, is generally admitted to be uncultured, I resent it very much that no stigma attaches to the gentleman who cannot do short division. I remember once at school having to do a piece of Latin prose about the Black Hole of Calcutta. It was a moving story as told in our prose book, and I had spent an interesting hour turning into fairly correct and wholly uninspired Latin – the sort of Latin I suppose which a small uneducated Roman child (who had heard the news) would have written to a schoolboy friend. The size of the Black Hole was given as 'twenty foot square'. I had no idea how to render this idiomatically, but I knew that a room 20 ft. square contained 400 square feet. Also I knew the Latin for one square foot. But you will not be surprised to hear that my form master, a man of culture and education, leapt upon me.

'Quadringenti,' he snapped, 'is 400, not 20.'

'Quite so,' I agreed. 'The room had 400 square feet.'

'Read it again. It says 20 square feet.'

'No, no, 20 feet square.'

He glared at me in indignation. 'What's the difference?' he said.

I sighed and began to explain. I went on explaining. If there had not been other things to do than teaching cultured and educated schoolmasters, I might be explaining still.

Yes, I resented this; and I resent now the matter-of-fact way in which we accept the ignorance of mathematics shown by our present teachers – the press. At every election in which there are only two candidates a dozen papers discover with amazement this astounding coincidence in the figures: that the decrease in, say, the Liberal vote subtracted from the increase in the Conservative vote is exactly equal to the increase in the poll. If there should happen to be three candidates for a seat, the coincidences discovered are yet more numerous and astonishing. Last Christmas a paper let itself go still further, and dived into the economics of the plum pudding. A plum pudding contains raisins, flour, and sugar. Raisins had gone up 2d. a pound, or whatever it was, flour 6d., and sugar 1d. Hence the pudding now would cost 9d. a pound more!

Consider, too, the extraordinary antics of the press over the methods of scoring in the cricket championship. Wonderful new suggestions are made which, if followed, could only have the effect of bringing the teams out in exactly the same order as before. The simplest of simple problems in algebra would have shown them this, but they feared to mix themselves up with such unknown powers of darkness. The Theory of Probability, again, leaves the press entirely cold, so that it is ready to father any childish 'system' for Monte Carlo. And nine men out of ten really believe that, if you toss a penny five times in the air and it comes down heads each time, it is more likely to come down tails than heads next time.

Yet papers and people who think like this are considered quite capable of dealing with the extra-ordinarily complicated figures of national finance. They may boom or condemn insurance bills and fiscal policies, and we listen to them reverently. As long as they know what Mr Gladstone said in '74, it doesn't seem to matter at all what Mr Todhunter said in his 'Arithmetic for Beginners'.

– The Charm of Golf –

W hen he reads of the notable doings of famous golfers, the eighteen-handicap man has no envy in his heart. For by this time he has discovered the great secret of golf. Before he began to play he wondered wherein lay the fascination of it; now he knows. Golf is so popular simply because it is the best game in the world at which to be bad.

Consider what it is to be bad at cricket. You have bought a new bat, perfect in balance; a new pair of pads, white as driven snow; gloves of the very latest design. Do they let you use them? No. After one ball, in the negotiation of which neither your bat, nor your pads, nor your gloves came into play, they send you back into the pavilion to spend the rest of the afternoon listening to fatuous stories of some old gentleman who knew Fuller Filch. And when your side takes the field, where are you? Probably at long leg both ends, exposed to the public gaze as the worst fieldsman in London. How devastating are your emotions. Remorse, anger, mortification, fill your heart; above all, envy – envy of the lucky immortals who disport themselves on the green level of Lord's.

Consider what it is to be bad at lawn tennis. True, you are allowed to hold on to your new racket all through the game, but how often are you allowed to employ it usefully? How often does your partner cry 'Mine!' and bundle you out of the way? Is there pleasure in playing football badly? You may spend the full eighty minutes in your new boots, but your relations with the ball will be distant. They do not give you a ball to yourself at football.

But how different a game is golf. At golf it is the bad player who gets the most strokes. However good his opponent, the bad player has the right to play out each hole to the end; he will get more than his share of the game. He need have no fears that his new driver will not be employed. He will have as many swings with it as the scratch man; more, if he misses the ball altogether upon one or two tees. If he buys a new niblick he is certain to get fun out of it on the very first day.

And, above all, there is this to be said for golfing mediocrity – the bad player can make the strokes of the good player. The poor cricketer has perhaps never made fifty in his life; as soon as he stands at the wickets he knows that he is not going to make fifty today. But the eighteen-handicap man has some time or other played every hole on the course to perfection. He has driven a ball 250 yards; he has made superb approaches; he has run down the long putt. Any of these things may suddenly happen to him again. And therefore it is not his fate to have to sit in the club smoking-room after his second round and listen to the wonderful deeds of others. He can join in too. He can say with perfect truth, 'I once carried the ditch at the fourth with my second,' or 'I remember when I drove into the bunker guarding the eighth green,' or even 'I did a three at the eleventh this afternoon' – bogey being five. But if the bad cricketer says, 'I remember when I took a century in forty minutes off Lockwood and Richardson,' he is nothing but a liar.

For these and other reasons golf is the best game in the world for the bad player. And sometimes I am tempted to go further and say that it is a better game for the bad player than for the good player. The joy of driving a ball straight after a week of slicing, the joy of putting a mashie shot dead, the joy of even a moderate stroke with a brassie; best of all, the joy of the perfect cleek shot – these things the good player will never know. Every stroke we bad players make we make in hope. It is never so bad but it might have been worse; it is never so bad but we are confident of doing better next time. And if the next stroke is good, what happiness fills our soul. How eagerly we tell ourselves that in a little while all our strokes will be as good.

What does Vardon know of this? If he does a five hole in four he blames himself that he did not do it in three; if he does it in five he is miserable. He will never experience that happy surprise with which we hail our best strokes. Only his bad strokes surprise him, and then we may suppose that he is not happy. His length and accuracy are mechanical; they are not the result, as so often in our case, of some suddenly applied maxim or some suddenly discovered innovation. The only thing which can vary in his game is his putting, and putting is not golf but croquet.

But of course we, too, are going to be as good as Vardon one day. We are only postponing the day because meanwhile it is so pleasant to be bad. And it is part of the charm of being bad at golf that in a moment, in a single night, we may become good. If the bad cricketer said to a good cricketer, 'What am I doing wrong?' the only possible answer would be, 'Nothing particular, except that you can't play cricket.' But if you or I were to say to our scratch friend, 'What am I doing wrong?' he would reply at once, 'Moving the head' or 'Dropping the right knee' or 'Not getting the wrists in soon enough', and by tomorrow we should be different players. Upon such a little depends, or seems to the eighteen-handicap to depend, excellence in golf.

And so, perfectly happy in our present badness and perfectly confident of our future goodness, we long-handicap men remain. Perhaps it would be pleasanter to be a little more certain of getting the ball safely off the first tee; perhaps at the fourteenth hole, where there is a right of way and the public encroach, we should like to feel that we have done with topping; perhaps –

Well, perhaps we might get our handicap down to fifteen this summer. But no lower; certainly no lower.

– A Question of Form –

T he latest invention on the market is the wasp gun.
In theory it is something like a letter clip; you
pull the trigger and the upper and lower plates snap
together with a suddenness which would surprise any
insect in between. The trouble will be to get him in the
right place before firing. But I can see that a lot of fun
can be got out of a wasp drive. We shall stand on the
edge of the marmalade while the beaters go through
it, and, given sufficient guns, there will not be many
insects to escape. A loader to clean the weapon at regular intervals will be a necessity.

Yet I am afraid that society will look down upon
the wasp gun. Anything useful and handy is always
barred by the best people. I can imagine a bounder
being described as 'the sort of person who uses a wasp
gun instead of a teaspoon'. As we all know, a hat-guard
is the mark of a very low fellow. I suppose the idea
is that you and I, being so dashed rich, do not much
mind if our straw hat does blow off into the Serpen-
tine; it is only the poor wretch of a clerk, unable to
afford a new one every day, who must take precautions
against losing his first. Yet how neat, how useful, is
the hat-guard. With what pride its inventor must have
given birth to it. Probably he expected a statue at the

corner of Cromwell Road, fitting reward for a public benefactor. He did not understand that, since his
invention was useful, it was probably bad form.

Consider, again, the Richard or 'dicky'. Could
there be anything neater or more dressy, anything
more thoroughly useful? Yet you and I scorn to wear
one. I remember a terrible situation in a story by Mr
W. S. Jackson. The hero found himself in a foreign
hotel without his luggage. To that hotel came, with
her father, the girl whom he adored silently. An invitation was given him to dinner with them, and he had
to borrow what clothes he could from friendly wait-
ers. These, alas! included a dicky. Well, the dinner
began well; our hero made an excellent impression;
all was gaiety. Suddenly a candle was overturned and
the flame caught the heroine's frock. The hero knew
what the emergency demanded. He knew how heroes
always whipped off their coats and wrapped them
round burning heroines. He jumped up like a bullet
(or whatever jumps up quickest) and ‒ remembered.

He had a dicky on! Without his coat, he would discover the dicky to the one person of all from whom he
wished to hide it. Yet if he kept his coat on, she might
die. A truly horrible dilemma. I forget which horn he
impaled himself upon, but I expect you and I would
have kept the secret of the Richard at all costs. And
what really is wrong with a false shirt-front? Nothing
except that it betrays the poverty of the wearer. Laun-
dry bills don't worry us, bless you, who have a new

straw hat every day; but how terrible if it was suspected that they did.

Our gentlemanly objection to the made-up tie seems to rest on a different foundation; I am doubtful as to the psychology of that. Of course it is a deception, but a deception is only serious when it passes itself off as something which really matters. Nobody thinks that a self-tied tie matters; nobody is really proud of being able to make a cravat out of a length of silk. I suppose it is simply the fact that a made-up tie saves time which condemns it; the safety razor was nearly condemned for a like reason. We of the leisured classes can spend hours over our toilet; by all means let us despise those who cannot.

As far as dress goes, a man only knows the things which a man mustn't do. It would be interesting if women would tell us what no real lady ever does. I have heard a woman classified contemptuously as one who does her hair up with two hair-pins, and no doubt bad feminine form can be observed in other shocking directions. But again it seems to be that the semblance of poverty, whether of means or of leisure, is the one thing which must be avoided.

Why, then, should the wasp gun be considered bad form? I don't know, but I have an instinctive feeling that it will be. Perhaps a wasp gun indicates a lack of silver spoons suitable for lethal uses. Perhaps it shows too careful a consideration of the marma-lade. A man of money drowns his wasp in the jar with his spoon, and carelessly calls for another pot to be opened. The poor man waits on the outskirts with his gun, and the marmalade, void of corpses, can still be passed round. Your gun proclaims your poverty; then let it be avoided.

All the same I think I shall have one. I have kept clear of hat-guards and Richards and made-up ties without quite knowing why, but honestly I have not felt the loss of them. The wasp gun is different; having seen it, I feel that I should be miserable without it. It is going to be excellent sport, wasp-shooting; a steady hand, a good eye, and a certain amount of courage will be called for. When the season opens I shall be there, good form or bad form. We shall shoot the apple-quince coverts first. 'Hornet over!'

– Superstition –

I have just read a serious column on the prospects for next year. This article consisted of contributions from experts in the various branches of industry (including one from a meteorological expert who, I need hardly tell you, forecasted a wet summer) and ended with a general summing up of the year by Old Moore or one of the minor prophets. Old Moore, I am sorry to say, left me cold.

I should like to believe in astrology, but I cannot. I should like to believe that the heavenly bodies sort themselves into certain positions in order that Zadkiel may be kept in touch with the future; the idea of a star whizzing a million miles out of its path by way of indicating a 'sensational divorce case in high life' is extraordinarily massive. But, candidly, I do not believe the stars bother. What the stars are for, what they are like when you get there, I do not know; but a starry night would not be so beautiful if it were simply meant as a warning to some unpleasant financier that Kaffirs were going up. The ordinary man looks at the heavens and thinks what an insignificant atom he is beneath them; the believer in astrology looks up and realizes afresh his overwhelming importance. Perhaps, after all, I am glad I do not believe.

Life must be a very tricky thing for the superstitious. At dinner a night or two ago I happened to say that I had never been in danger of drowning. I am not sure now that it was true, but I still think that it was harmless. However, before I had time to elaborate my theme (whatever it was) I was peremptorily ordered to touch wood. I protested that both my feet were on the polished oak and both my elbows on the polished mahogany (one always knew that *some* good instinct inspired the pleasant habit of elbows on the table) and that anyhow I did not see the need. However, because one must not argue at dinner I tapped the table two or three times . . . and now I suppose I am immune. At the same time I should like to know exactly whom I have appeased.

For this must be the idea of the wood-touching superstition, that a malignant spirit dogs one's conversational footsteps, listening eagerly for the complacent word. 'I have never had the mumps,' you say airily. 'Ha, ha!' says the spirit, 'haven't you? Just you wait till next Tuesday, my boy.' Unconsciously we are crediting Fate with our own human weaknesses. If a man standing on the edge of a pond said aloud, 'I have never fallen into a pond in my life', and we happened to be just behind him, the temptation to push him in would be irresistible. Irresistible, that is by us; but it is charitable to assume that Providence can control itself by now.

Of course, nobody really thinks that our good or evil spirits have any particular feeling about wood, that they like it stroked; nobody, I suppose, not even the most superstitious, really thinks that Fate is especially touchy in the matter of salt and ladders. Equally, of course, many people who throw spilt salt over their left shoulders are not superstitious in the least, and are only concerned to display that readiness in the face of any social emergency which is said to be the mark of good manners. But there are certainly many who feel that it is the part of a wise man to propitiate the unknown, to bend before the forces which work for harm; and they pay tribute to Fate by means of these little customs in the hope that they will secure in return an immunity from evil. The tribute is nominal, but it is an acknowledgment all the same.

A proper sense of proportion leaves no room for superstition. A man says, 'I have never been in a shipwreck', and becoming nervous touches wood. Why is he nervous? He has this paragraph before his eyes: 'Among the deceased was Mr —. By a remarkable coincidence this gentleman had been saying only a few days before that he had never been in a shipwreck. Little did he think that his next voyage would falsify his words so tragically.' It occurs to him that he has read paragraphs like that again and again. Perhaps he has. Certainly he has never read a paragraph like this: 'Among the deceased was Mr —. By a remarkable coincidence this gentleman had never made the remark that he had not yet been in a shipwreck.' Yet that paragraph could have been written truthfully thousands of times. A sense of proportion would tell you that if only one side of a case is ever recorded, that side acquires an undue importance.

The truth is that Fate does not go out of its way to be dramatic. If you or I had the power of life and death in our hands, we should no doubt arrange some remarkably bright and telling effects. A man who spilt the salt callously would be drowned next week in the Dead Sea, and a couple who married in May would expire simultaneously in the May following. But Fate cannot worry to think out all the clever things that we should think out. It goes about its business solidly and unromantically, and by the ordinary laws of chance it achieves every now and then something startling and romantic. Superstition thrives on the fact that only the accidental dramas are reported.

But there are charms to secure happiness as well as charms to avert evil. In these I am a firm believer. I do not mean that I believe that a horseshoe hung up in the house will bring me good luck; I mean that if anybody does believe this, then the hanging up of his horseshoe will probably bring him good luck. For if you believe that you are going to be lucky, you go about your business with a smile, you take disaster with a smile, you start afresh with a smile. And to do that is to be in the way of happiness.

– Spiritualism and the Value
of Evidence –

I t seems to be impossible nowadays to write about spiritualism without bringing in the names of its two principal champions: Sir Oliver Lodge and Sir Arthur Conan Doyle. It is appropriate that this should be so, for these two names can be taken as representative of Science and Faith, in between which Spiritualism stands uncertainly, waiting to declare itself. If it is a Science, does not the name of Sir Oliver Lodge carry weight? It does. If it is a Faith, does not the self-sacrifice of Sir Arthur compel belief? It does. But, on the other hand, if it is a Faith, then Sir Oliver Lodge's adherence to it means no more than that of any other man, and less than that of some poor outcast in the slums; and if it is a Science, then the fanatic faith of Sir Arthur is entirely out of place. Who, then, is to be our antagonist? What are we discussing? A Science or a Faith? This is our first difficulty.

Christianity is a Faith; we believe in it, or not. Vaccination is a Science; we believe in it, or not. But the two beliefs are different. In the one case we believe, or doubt, with our hearts; in the other case with our minds. The proofs of Christianity are subjective and spiritual, the proofs of vaccination are objective and material. An anti-vaccinationist, who has not made a faith of his belief, could be converted by overwhelming proof, if such were available, but the anti-Christian can only convert himself.

Now, is Spiritualism offered to us as an extension of the physical laws of the universe, of which we seem to know some, yet of others remain in deepest ignorance; or is it offered to us as a religion, giving us in the greatest degree that hope and that comfort without which the universe itself becomes unthinkable? Faith, says Saint Paul, is the substance of things hoped for, the evidence of things not seen. If Spiritualism is a faith, no words could more truly describe that faith. 'The substance of things hoped for.' It is enough for the believer to proclaim that this is what he hopes for; it is enough for the unbeliever to reply that he hopes for something other. Neither is required to justify himself. No argument is possible between them. But if Spiritualism is a manifestation of certain laws of nature for which authority is now claimed, then the unbeliever may sit in judgement on that claim. He may demand, and consider the evidence.

Let us first regard Spiritualism as a Science, and consider the evidence for it.

Now the value of evidence depends upon the credibility of the witness. Spiritualists make the mistake of thinking that it depends upon the honesty of the witness. Over and over again we are told that this and that distinguished man and woman attended a séance and witnessed remarkable things. How can we possibly doubt their word as to what took place? Well, the honesty of the Pope may be considered above suspicion. We could not doubt his word. But if the Pope told us that he had seen a woman having an epileptic fit on the steps of St Paul's at eleven o'clock in the morning, we should not consider the fact therefore established. We should ask ourselves the following questions:

1. How does he know that it was not a man dressed up as a woman?

2. Does he know the difference between epilepsy and other kinds of fits?

3. Is he acquainted with St Paul's, or has he perhaps confused it with Westminster Abbey?

4. Did he guess the time, or consult a watch or clock?

5. Is that watch or clock accurate?

We see, in short, that whether we accept or reject the evidence does not depend in the least on the honesty of the witness. We may trust a man's honour but remain doubtful of his medical skill, his knowledge of London and the works of his watch.

But should we, in fact, so dispute the Pope's story? No. We should not dispute it, for the reason that the story is in itself credible, and not worth disputing. If the most irresponsible man of my acquaintance tells me that he has just seen Hobbs make a century at the Oval in two and a half hours, I am ready to believe him; but if my most accurate friend tells me that he has just seen G. K. Chesterton make a century at Lord's in ten minutes, I shall assume that he is under an hallucination. The first statement is natural and credible; the second unnatural and incredible.

So it comes to this. We believe the evidence we are ready to believe, and reject the evidence we are not ready to believe. But if this is true of us who receive the evidence of Spiritualism at second-hand, it is equally true of those Spiritualists who have received it at first hand. The man who urgently wants to receive a message from his dead son will believe that he is receiving a message from his dead son; it is so easy for him.

The Spiritualist has been known to deny this; to say that he had no prepossessions either way when he began investigating. Often he claims that he was actually a sceptic – until he was convinced. It is worth while to consider just what a Spiritualist means in this case by scepticism.

I go out to dinner and am entertained afterwards by a conjuror. He performs a remarkable trick. He gives me two cards out of an authenticated pack, and lets me hide them. Then he shuffles the cards and invites me to turn up the top two. They are the two which I have just hidden. Marvellous! I go home and tell Smith about it. Smith is a complete sceptic. He does not doubt my honesty, but says that I have been deceived in some way; it was a trick pack; or the conjuror had extra cards up his sleeve; or he got to my hiding place when my back was turned. Something. The more I assure him

that none of these things happened, the more sceptical he remains. He is certain that the conjuror could
not bring the trick off in his presence. So I arrange
that he shall try. The trick begins, with Smith taking
every precaution which suggests itself to him. The two
cards, let us say, are the eight of hearts and the nine
of diamonds. When all the preliminaries are over, the
conjuror with a confident smile invites Smith to turn
up the top two cards . . .

And what does this confirmed sceptic suppose he
is going to see when he turns up the cards? The four of
clubs and the King of spades? A couple of Queens? Of
course not. Yet if he is a confirmed sceptic, this is what
he should expect. But he doesn't expect it, because at
the moment of turning he is no longer sceptical. He is
at that moment absolutely certain that in some miraculous way the hidden cards will be there; the eight of
hearts and the nine of diamonds. 'And, by Heaven,' he
cries, 'so they are.'

But they are not. That, in fact, is the trick. The
cards now turned up are the nine of hearts and the
eight of diamonds; but so habitually inaccurate are we
all, and so easily blinded by a preconceived belief, that
in every case the eight of diamonds and the nine of
hearts will be mistaken for the nine of diamonds and
the eight of hearts. To the good conjuror there is no
such thing as a sceptic. Scepticism always gives way at
the critical moment.

Or rather, it appears to give way then, but it has

really given way before. Try to imagine for yourself the dialogue between an anguished and adoring mother and the alleged spirit of her dead son, a dialogue in which the mother remains coldly on the defensive, answering 'Sir' to the voice's 'Mummy darling', until it has identified the hiding place of the dead rabbit, or told her to look in the left hand cupboard in the box-room for his old tennis-shoes; whereupon she apologizes and calls him 'Dearest'. It is inconceivable.

Evidence, then, of manifestations which in themselves seem barely credible, and which come to us through witnesses themselves not entirely credible, is not evidence which carries conviction. Is there no evidence which would be more likely to convince us? For myself, I should prefer spiritual evidence; evidence, that is, of the spiritual presence of the dead, rather than material evidence (table-rappings and what not) of the material presence of the dead. I mentioned this preference of mine once in an article written for the Daily News, and was promptly provided with the evidence which I wanted. It was a poem by Dryden which had just come through from the next world; a poem by one who was a great poet in his lifetime, and who now had two hundred years' knowledge of unearthly beauty to add to his earthly knowledge. All he could do with this equipment was a verse such as one might find in a schoolgirl's magazine, in which 'earth' rhymed to 'turf'. When I commented on this, I was told scornfully that, even in such worldly matters as telephonings, the operators were not always accurate; not inhumanly accurate; and that a medium was merely a very human transmitter. True, I was a very human transmitter myself once; a signaller in the Army. I admit with shame that, taking down a preface of Bernard Shaw's on the buzzer at twenty words a minute, I might have done him some injustice . . . but I doubt if the result would have looked like a short story by Miss Ethel M. Dell. Nor was a communication from Longfellow, sent to me through the same medium, more convincing. Seventy years after his death Longfellow was apparently still writing in the Hiawatha metre. I am sorry, but, speaking as an expert, I say that the one certain fact in this uncertain universe is that Longfellow isn't. There may be a million people in Heaven writing in the Hiawatha, metre but Longfellow is not one of them. That is absolutely certain. I may know nothing about Spiritualism, but I know something about writing. One doesn't. One simply doesn't.

This, it may be said, is trivial. It is. But it is also symptomatic. Perhaps my chief objection to the Spiritualists' creed is that acceptance of it seems to mean the dethronement of reason. A medium is caught cheating. Does the spiritualist reject him? No. He assures us that the medium was a perfectly honest medium – until he was caught cheating; that the strain of being a medium is very great; that many of the best mediums have to take to drink – and cheating. Indeed, the fact that he was caught cheating is almost proof that until that moment he was the most honest of mediums . . . The doubter goes to a séance hoping for proof. He is not satisfied with the proof which he gets. That is because he doubted and created an atmosphere of distrust, in which, as is well known, it is impossible for spirits to manifest themselves; so that even his dissatisfaction is in itself a proof . . . and so on.

As a Science, then, Spiritualism seems to me just a little unscientific. Do I like it any better as a Faith? I do not believe in Spiritualism as a Faith, for the simple and sound reason that I do not want to. It does not offer me the evidence of things hoped for.

It is a little difficult to know exactly what it does offer, for the Spiritualist's picture of Heaven is varied. It is also a little difficult not to be ribald about some of the pictures which are drawn. It is, of course, easy, and not always helpful, to be ribald about somebody else's religion. The old Christian idea of Heaven as a place wherein one perpetually played the harp in one's nightgown offered similar opportunities. Yet ribaldry sometimes has its value. Christianity has not suffered by discarding whatever offered a target for the mockers.

The essence of the Spiritualist's creed is that there are no dead. I am afraid that I get no comfort from this assurance. To call death a passing does not make it any less bitter. It is to me merely stupid to offer that contact with the dead which the Spiritualists profess to give us as a tolerable substitute for that contact with the living which we enjoy in this world. Even that spiritual contact which Sir Arthur offers us in the next world gives me no firm foundation for faith. He tells us that time moves on in the next world contemporaneously with this; that a mother who loses her baby, a girl of three years old, and dies herself fifteen years later, will find a daughter of eighteen waiting to welcome her. The only possible question I can ask is: Why on earth or in Heaven should she want a strange daughter of eighteen?

Sir Arthur also tells us – much, if I may say so respectfully, as a showman trying to do the best for his public – that if we die old and decrepit, we find ourselves in the next world in our prime. Speaking for myself, I should like a little further assurance as to who is to decide what is my prime. Authors, in particular, are often told by their critics that they are no longer what they were. We do not always agree with our critics. Moreover, our intellectual prime, whenever it may be, rarely coincides with our physical prime. The next world is apparently physical as well as spiritual. The physical side seems to stop short at digestion and pro-creation, being rather more of a silhouette than any-thing; but, according to the Spiritualists, it is there, and we should want to make the best of it. But shall I really have survived, if I survive in a combination of body and mind which is not myself at all: which has never been in this world, and could never be recog-nized in the next?

If I find this new world hard to realize and unattractive to consider, it is because all my hopes of another world are of a world more beautiful than anything I can imagine in this one. To think of the infinite in terms of the finite is beyond me. I feel myself as little competent to imagine the next world as to explain this. Nor do I demand of my Faith an infinity of existence in either. All I can ask is that some day, if only in one blinding moment, I may understand; all I can hope is that, when that moment comes, I may leave behind me in this world something which will not wholly be forgotten.

– Age –

As I was saying a little while ago, I am on the verge of seventy, and don't feel it. Somebody (it may have been myself) put out the ingenious theory that the reason why actors and actresses continue to look so young is because the hours when they are being Julius Caesar or Little Lord Fauntleroy are no part of their own lives, and so do not age them. Thus an actor who had played Hamlet for eight performances a week throughout the year would himself have lived only forty-five weeks, assuming that he kept his mind on his part during the dressing-room intervals. Continuous employment would give him back one year in eight. Now that I have worked it out, I can see that the theory is not very sound; for an actor is far from being in continuous employment, and even if he were, he would only look forty-two when he was forty-eight, which anybody can do.

But it might apply to a novelist, who does live continuously the lives of others, and perhaps only grows old in the night. It is more likely, however, that the reason why a writer does not easily acquire the dignity and authority of old age is that he is never in a position of dignity or authority. Indeed, he never gets beyond the apprentice stage. When judges, clergymen and schoolmasters open their lips, no dog can bark. Not that any dog wants to; it is assumed (a little too readily, perhaps,) that a Judge knows all about the law, a clergyman all about God, and a schoolmaster all about the subject he is teaching. But however long a writer has been in the business, he is still without authority for anybody but himself. All he knows is how to write in his own way. He will never be Sir Oracle, and any dog can bark at him.

When I wrote an autobiography twelve years ago, I called it *It's Too Late Now*, meaning that it was too late then to be any other sort of writer; no doubt at 106 it will still be too late. The American editor who published it in monthly instalments altered the title. This is a habit of American editors.

I fancy that the Oath of Installation – taken (as I see it) in shirt sleeves, elastically banded, with blue pencil upheld in right hand – ends, 'And I do solemnly swear that, whatever the author shall have called any story, article or poem submitted to me, and however suitable his title shall be, I will immediately alter it to one of my own choosing, thus asserting by a single stroke the dignity of my office and my own independence.' However this may be, the autobiography was re-titled *What Luck!*

I was annoyed with the Editor at the time; but looking back on my life from what I suppose I must call early middle age, I am inclined now to agree with him.

PEACEFUL LIFE

– Men at Arms –

This morning I came across a letter which I had written on October 13th, 1916, from what was left of a French village called Bully-Grenay. My C.O. was a man for whom I had the greatest admiration, and when he died between the wars, I paid a farewell tribute to him in The Times. He had a delightfully ironic humour, of which I gave one or two examples, reminding myself of them by referring to letters which I had written home. This one, however, had escaped me, until today.

There was a certain newly-joined subaltern, a hard-working but extremely unattractive youth, whom I described as 'dry-dirty', whatever that meant. The Colonel and the Adjutant were talking about him in the H.Q. Mess, to which as Signalling Officer I belonged; and the Adjutant said in his kindly way that he was 'a very well-meaning boy, but not exactly a leader.'

'No,' said the Colonel, 'the men would never follow him – except out of curiosity.'

– The Honour of Your Country –

We were resting after the first battle of the Somme. Naturally all the talk in the Mess was of after-the-war. Ours was the H.Q. Mess, and I was the only subaltern; the youngest of us was well over thirty. With a gravity befitting our years and (except for myself) our rank, we discussed not only restaurants and revues, but also Reconstruction.

The Colonel's idea of Reconstruction included a large army of conscripts. He did not call them conscripts. The fact that he had chosen to be a soldier himself, out of all the professions open to him, made it difficult for him to understand why a million others should not do the same without compulsion. At any rate, we must have the men. The one thing the war had taught us was that we must have a real Continental army.

I asked why. 'Theirs not to reason why' on parade, but in the H.Q. Mess on active service the Colonel is a fellow human being. So I asked him why we wanted a large army after the war.

For the moment he was at a loss. Of course, he might have said 'Germany', had it not been decided already that there would be no Germany after the war. He did not like to say 'France', seeing that we were

even then enjoying the hospitality of the most delightful of French villages. So, after a little hesitation, he
said 'Spain'.

A t least he put it like this:

'Of course, we must have an army, a large army.'

'But why?' I said again.

'How else can you – can you defend the honour of
your country?'

'The Navy.'

'The Navy! Pooh! The Navy isn't a weapon of
attack; it's a weapon of defence.'

'But you said "defend". '

'Attack,' put in the Major oracularly, 'is the best
defence.'

'Exactly.'

I hinted at the possibilities of blockade. The
Colonel was scornful. 'Sitting down under an insult
for months and months,' he called it, until you starved
the enemy into surrender. He wanted something much
more picturesque, more immediately effective than
that. (Something, presumably, more like the Somme.)

'But give me an example,' I said, 'of what you mean
by "insults" and "honour".'

Whereupon he gave me this extraordinary example of the need for a large army.

'Well, supposing,' he said, 'that fifty English
women in Madrid were suddenly murdered, what
would you do?'

I thought for a moment, and then said that I should

probably decide not to take my wife to Madrid until things had settled down a bit.

'I'm supposing that you're Prime Minister,' said the Colonel, a little annoyed. 'What is England going to do?'

'Ah! . . . Well, one might do nothing. After all, what *is* one to do? One can't restore them to life.'

The Colonel, the Major, even the Adjutant, expressed his contempt for such a cowardly policy. So I tried again.

'Well,' I said, 'I might decide to murder fifty Spanish women in London, just to even things up.'

The Adjutant laughed. But the Colonel was taking it too seriously for that.

'Do you mean it?' he asked.

'Well, what would *you* do, sir?'

'Land an army in Spain,' he said promptly, 'and show them what it meant to treat English women like that.'

'I see. They would resist of course?'

'No doubt.'

'Yes. But equally without doubt we should win in the end?'

'Certainly.'

'And so re-establish England's honour.'

'Quite so.'

'I see. Well, sir, I really think my way is the better. To avenge the fifty murdered English women, you are going to kill (say) 100,000 Spaniards who have had no connexion with the murders, and 50,000 English-men who are even less concerned. Indirectly also you will cause the death of hundreds of guiltless Spanish women and children, besides destroying the happiness of thousands of English wives and mothers. Surely my way – of murdering only fifty innocents – is just as effective and much more humane.'

'That's nonsense,' said the Colonel shortly.

'And the other is war.'

We were silent for a little, and then the Colonel poured himself out a whisky.

'All the same,' he said, as he went back to his seat, 'you haven't answered my question.'

'What was that, sir?'

'What you would do in the case I mentioned. Seri-ously.'

'Oh! Well, I stick to my first answer. I would do nothing – except, of course, ask for an explanation and an apology. If you *can* apologize for that sort of thing.'

'And if they were refused?'

'Have no more official relations with Spain.'

'That's all you would do?'

'Yes.'

'And you think that that is consistent with the honour of a great nation like England?'

'Perfectly.'

'Oh! Well, I don't.'

An indignant silence followed.

'May I ask *you* a question now, sir?' I said at last.

'Well?'

'Suppose this time England begins. Suppose we murder all the Spanish women in London first. What are you going to do – as Spanish Premier?'

'Er – I don't quite –'

'Are you going to order the Spanish Fleet to sail for the mouth of the Thames, and hurl itself upon the British fleet?'

'Of course not. She has no fleet.'

'Then do you agree with the – er Spanish Colonel who goes about saying that Spain's honour will never be safe until she has a fleet as big as England's?'

'That's ridiculous. They couldn't possibly.'

'Then what *could* Spain do in the circumstances?'

'Well, she – er – she could – er – protest.'

'And would that be consistent with the honour of a small nation like Spain?'

'In the circumstances,' said the Colonel unwillingly, 'er – yes.'

'So that what it comes to is this. Honour only demands that you should attack the other man if you are much bigger than he is. When a man insults my wife, I look him carefully over; if he is a stone heavier than I, then I satisfy my honour by a mild protest. But if he only has one leg, and is three stone lighter, honour demands that I should jump on him.'

'We're talking of nations,' said the Colonel gruffly, 'not of men. It's a question of prestige.'

'Which would be increased by a victory over Spain?'

The Major began to get nervous. After all, I was only a subaltern. He tried to cool the atmosphere a little.

'I don't know why poor old Spain should be dragged into it like this,' he said, with a laugh. 'I had a very jolly time in Madrid years ago.'

'Oh, I only gave Spain as an example,' said the Colonel casually.

'It might just as well have been Switzerland?' I suggested.

There was silence for a little.

'Talking of Switzerland –' I said, as I knocked out my pipe.

'Oh, go on,' said the Colonel, with a good-humoured shrug. 'I've brought this on myself.'

'Well, sir, what I was wondering was – What would happen to the honour of England if fifty English women were murdered at Interlaken?'

The Colonel was silent.

'However large an army we had –' I went on.

The Colonel struck a match.

'It's a funny thing, honour,' I said. 'And prestige.'

The Colonel pulled at his pipe.

'Just fancy,' I murmured, 'the Swiss can do what they like to British subjects in Switzerland, and we can't get at them. Yet England's honour does not suffer, the world is no worse a place to live in, and one can spend quite a safe holiday at Interlaken.'

'I remember being there in '94,' began the Major hastily . . .

– King and Country –

W ars may be declared for economic reasons, but they are fought by volunteers for sentimental reasons. However loudly an iron-field may call to the Elder Statesman, the call will come to Youth through the voices of King and Country. And even the most cynical statesman would hesitate to tell the young volunteer that his King and Country needed him in order to make a certain corner of the world safe for speculators.

But are wars even declared entirely for economic reasons? Is not the statesman also subject to the sentimental impulse? If his motives were purely economic, one would expect him to make out a balance-sheet before he issued his ultimatum; taking into account, on the credit side the value of the oil-fields, gold-fields, iron-fields, or whatever was the gleam which he was following; and, on the debit side, the probable length of the war, the estimated cost per day, the estimated number of casualties (and consequent cost of pensions), depreciation of stock, insurance against defeat, damage inflicted by aeroplanes, and so forth. He makes no such balance-sheet. It may be said that he hopes to get his expenses back by way of indemnity, just as a suitor in the law-courts hopes to get his costs. Well, he has discovered by now that indemnity on that scale is simply unpayable; but, even before this great and (one would have thought) elementary discovery was made, there still remained, on the debit side of the account, the irreplaceable human lives. Are the economic gains of war ever balanced against dead Englishmen? Against human misery? It would hardly seem so. The economics of the war-minded statesman are the economics of the nursery. A baby putting its hand into the fire to take out the pretty coal shows as much awareness of reality.

For the truth is this. A nation may declare war in pursuit of some material end, yet, in reality, it is declaring war at the call of 'honour'. Because *'honour' demands that a nation shall achieve its ends regardless of cost.*

This 'honour', as I have shown, is nothing honourable. It is merely the artificial pride of the duellist. In the days when duelling was the fashion men fought because they 'had to fight'; because honour compelled them to fight; because they were too proud not to fight.

Now it is almost impossible for Pacifist and Militarist to get into argument about war without the analogy of the duel being brought up, sooner or later, by one or other of them. It might be as well, then, now that I have likened the motive of war to the motive of the duel, to follow the analogy through to the end.

Twenty years ago the comparison between private

war and international war was often made. 'Consider', the pacifist's argument ran, 'how ridiculous the idea of abolishing duelling must have seemed once – as ridiculous as seems now the idea of abolishing war. But the world progresses; and if we have got rid of the one, why should we not get rid of the other?' To which came the inevitable militarist answer: 'We got rid of duelling because we had an over-riding authority which could call duellists to account; but it is impossible to create an over-riding authority which can call nations to account.'

Since those days the League of Nations was conceived, has come into being, and now waits uncertainly on its future.

Yet the argument remains. And the argument is not: Since national law has enforced the abandonment of duelling, therefore international law could enforce the abandonment of war; but simply: Since we have outgrown the one convention, is there any reason why we should not outgrow the other?

It is true that, if I fight a duel with a man who has insulted me, I shall be put in prison, and that if I kill him, I shall be hanged; it is true that, however much I wanted to fight him, the certainty of imprisonment, and the probability that one way or the other I should lose my own life, would prevent me from challenging him. But the more profound truth is that I no longer want to fight him. And the reason that I do not want to fight him is not because I am afraid of the consequences, but because the whole idea of fighting seems now to be ridiculous. The duelling convention, in fact, has ceased to exist.

Is there any necessity for the war-convention to continue? We have outgrown the one convention, why should we not outgrow the other?

For this reason (says the Elder Statesman). There is always an intermediary period when an idea is not strong enough to flourish by itself, but needs protection; just as young grass needs protection in between the time when it is sown and the time when it is established. In the case of duelling this protection was given by the Law, and under the Law the idea that private war was wrong and foolish grew to its present strength. But in the case of international war we are back again at the old problem. By what Law, and by what sanctions, can we protect the idea of Peace until it is so firmly established in the minds of nations that international war seems both wicked and ridiculous?

– Pro Patria –

A nd then, on Armistice Day, there are the heroic dead to be commemorated. The usual speeches are made, the usual sermons preached, the usual leading articles written, and from every one of these threnodies, however pacific in intention, the suggestion escapes that to fight for one's country is the noblest form of self-expression, to die for one's country the noblest form of self-immolation. Our heroic dead, our immortal dead. Dulce et decorum est pro patria mori.

Yet, looking at the matter in the cold light of reason, we see that a man is not a hero who is conscripted; or who is in the army for lack of other employment; or who is carried away by the waving of flags and the thrumming of bands; or who joins up, as so many did, because life in wartime is hell anyway, and only in uniform can one escape from thinking about it. Nor, we observe, do these ordinary unheroic men become heroes just because an incompetent commander has hurled them in mass upon uncut wire, there to hang like blackberries until they are ripe for the honour, if Chance picks upon them, of Unknown Warrior. Alive or dead, they retain the nobility or ignobility of character which was theirs in peace-time; just as the young men of today, who have not yet had a war arranged for them, are noble and ignoble.

This sentimental feeling that war is an exhibition of heroism, which grants diplomas to all who attend it, is far from the truth. The whole conception of modern war is almost comically unheroic. Gone are the days of Agincourt when King Harry 'would not lose so great an honour as one man more from England would share from him'. Gone are the days when the little ships of England ranged themselves proudly, almost contemptuously, against the invincible Armada. Gone are the days when a fight was hardly a fight to an Englishman if the odds against him were less than three to one. Today, with no war in sight, yet in terror lest we should be outbuilt, we seek to match ship for ship, gun for gun, aeroplane for aeroplane; and even so, when the war comes, it will be the 'gentlemen in England', the chemists and the munition workers, upon whom victory will depend.

But though modern war is not heroic in itself, it might be urged that those who fall in war fall for a cause outside themselves, and, by so doing, have made, as the threnodists say, the supreme sacrifice: they have given their lives for others. Well, let us continue to be unsentimental. Self-sacrifice, to be heroic, must be a voluntary sacrifice and a deliberate sacrifice. Not more than 5 per cent of the soldiers in the last war volunteered to fight. Those who did volunteer went into action knowing that casualties would be suffered, but thinking and hoping and praying (so unheroic are the ordinary people who die in war) that the casualties would be, not to themselves but to their companions. They took the risk of death willingly, as young fools take it daily on motorbicycles, as men take it in aeroplanes, or in search of a Pole, or after big game, or among the mountains; but the absolute certainty of death is something far removed from this. A man is indeed a hero if, longing for life, he accepts death of his own will. How many heroes do we commemorate each year? How many of the 'immortal dead' have deliberately died for their country?

Neither in its origins nor in its conduct is war heroic. Splendidly heroic deeds are done in war, but not by those responsible for its conduct, and not exclusively and inevitably by the dead. Of the ten million men who were killed in the last war, more than nine million had to fight whether they wanted to or not, and of these nine million some eight million did nothing heroic whatever before they were killed. They are no more 'immortal' than a linen-draper who is run over by a lorry; their deaths were no more 'pleasant' and 'fitting' than the death of a stock-broker in his bath.

But of course one can't just say to a million mothers: 'I want your sons,' and then six months later; 'Sorry, they're all dead.' If war is to be made tolerable, the romantic tradition must be handed on. 'Madam, I took away your son, but I give you back the memory of a hero. Each year we will celebrate together his immortal passing. Dulce et decorum est pro patria mori.'

– Fighting for Peace –

W ars, however, are not always fought in pursuit or defence of territory. A 'tariff war' may lead to an ultimatum. Then which nation is attacking and which defending? In a sense each is defending its rights, for each will proclaim the right to live, and allege that the other is endangering it. Wars may be declared, as Austria declared war on Servia, in defence of some supposed prestige. It was generally admitted that Austria had the right to some sort of 'satisfaction' for the 'insult' of Serajevo, and it was, in fact, the clash between Austria's 'defence' of her original claim and Servia's 'defence' against an excessive claim which led to the Great War.

It is clear then, that, whatever the origin of a war, each country can protest that she is not the aggressor; each country can claim that she is 'resisting' an unfair demand, 'defending' her prestige, or 'repelling' an attack upon her rights. It is also clear that with the modern facilities for organizing and distributing lies, which every government possesses and none scruples to use, the justice of a cause can be firmly established in the minds of all nationals fighting for it. If the countries of Europe are going to limit themselves in the future to defensive wars; if they are going to limit themselves to wars for which God's approval has been obtained in advance by their clergy; they will not be pledged to one single war less. To justify defensive war is automatically to justify the next war in which one's own country is engaged, and is, therefore, automatically to justify war.

But there is another reason why any distinction made between aggressive and defensive preparations for war leaves no hope of peace. As I said in a previous chapter, no nation trusts the word of another nation. It is not surprising that statesmen should be cynical about the good faith of each other, when they have been given such abundant reason for cynicism. If there is one sin which brings its own punishment, it is the sin of lying. Truth is the supreme virtue, and it is because we have allowed politicians to neglect it at the call of a false patriotism that we have been burdened with this nightmare of war.

For it is the simple fact that no statesman, no general, has ever hesitated to lie if the good of the state seemed to demand it. When periodically there is an outcry against the sale of honours, every leader of every party blandly professes ignorance of such sale. They are lying; we know that they are lying; but it is not a matter of adverse comment. The convention is that their personal honour is untouched if the lies which they tell are in the interest of the state. When, in war, a general orders an attack which is repulsed with hideous losses, he announces that 'all goes well with

British arms'. It is a lie – but pro patria. 'I could not love thee, dear, so much, loved I not honour more', said Lovelace to his lady. Unfortunately no Patriot has ever addressed his country so.

This is traditional. Even in home politics, still more in international politics, the ordinary standards of honour have never applied. One could not imagine the craziest Patriot praying that his son should grow up 'as honourable as England'. International politics is a morass of treachery, theft, broken promises, lies, evasions, bluff, trickiness, bullying, deliberate misunderstanding and shabby attempts to get an opponent into a false position. Our whole conception of national morality is different from our conception of private morality. Consider, as one trivial example of this difference, the war-debt between England and America. If this had been a debt contracted between two honourable men in analogous circumstances, the one would have been as insistent on paying it as the other would have been scornful of accepting payment. As it is, we have an excited discussion, every six months or so, as to whether England should, or should not, keep her word. Imagine a similar discussion in a family which considered its honour to be above reproach!

Now we cannot have it both ways. We cannot disregard truth and expect to be trusted. By its lack of candour in the past every nation has surrendered to its enemies the right of interpretation of its actions. For England to maintain a large navy and a large air-force:

to asseverate that she is keeping them 'solely for defensive purposes': and to expect any other country to believe her is to exhibit an ingenuousness unworthy even of the nursery. Armaments in the hands of a foreign nation will always be aggressive armaments: partly because no faith is possible between statesmen who put their country above their honour; partly because, with the best faith in the world, there can never be agreement as to what is aggression and what defence.

– Put Out More Flags –

Nobody who heard on that September morning in 1939 the doleful voice of Neville Chamberlain, announcing that we were now at war with Germany, will ever forget it. A few, a very few, of those who heard it may have foreseen that the war would last nearly six years. Not one of them would have believed it possible that within two years of the end of it the fear of a new and more terrible war would be overshadowing the world.

I have been an ardent Pacifist since 1910, and still am. In my vocabulary a Pacifist is not the same as a Conscientious Objector. Nothing is gained by burying one's head in the sand when war breaks out, and supposing that it will pass one by. On the contrary, as long as one is alive one is taking part in the war, willingly or unwillingly, actively or passively, as a force or as a deadweight: that is, one is helping either one's country or the enemy. The only logical protest for a Conscientious Objector who refuses to take part is suicide; preferably at sea, so that the war effort shall not be interrupted by the need for burying the body.

A Pacifist, in my definition, is one who does not believe that war is 'a legitimate extension of policy' or 'a biological necessity' or 'human nature', and who does believe that its economic gains are illusory. So, since it results in the torture and death of innocent and harmless people, he is not only of opinion that it should be outlawed, but looks forward to a day when the whole world will share his opinion. Common sense and common decency, he tells himself, must surely prevail.

In 1910 Pacifism was derided. All the wars in the memory of Englishmen had taken place outside their country, and could be followed with the eager but impersonal interest with which we now follow the broadcast of a cricket match. It was true that a few soldiers got killed, but this was just an occupational risk, cheerfully to be accepted in return for the adventure and the glory promised. If the civilians did think about war in the abstract, they told themselves that it was bracing, like corporal punishment and cold baths; and that, since it had been going on for thousands of years, it would probably be wrong, and would certainly be impossible, to stop it now. So Pacifists were dismissed as idealists, cranks, and, as likely as not, vegetarians.

In 1920 nearly everybody in this country was a Pacifist in theory, and millions of them were Pacifists in practice: that is, they were trying and hoping, by means of the League of Nations, to make an end of war. This change of opinion was due, and due only, to the experience of a war much more terrible than any that they had known, and much nearer home; a war which had cast its shadow over nearly every family in the land.

By 1945 Pacifism was the accepted policy of the whole country. This was because, and only because, the destruction of so many lives, of so much beauty, in our own fortress, had blasted, for all and for ever, the old conventional beliefs.

But there were still a few in the world who believed that war could be used profitably for their own purposes. They were not to be found among the common people; nor in those countries whose Governments were chosen by the common people; but only in those countries where the common people are oppressed and silent, and where a few fools, a few criminals, can still falsify the conclusions of humanity. Fortunately for the rest of the world humanity now has the atom bomb, and on the subject of war the atom bomb will speak the last word.

The atom bomb is the final proof of what Norman Angell called the Great Illusion. He proved to the conviction of some of us in 1910 – a conviction which two World Wars have so enormously sustained and enlarged – the simple truth that a victorious war brings in no material dividends. This did not prove, of course, that there was nothing to be won by an aggressive war; for there are other gains in a Dictator's mind than economic ones. But all the aesthetic pleasure of a triumphal victory march across Europe, Hammer and Sickle waving with the cohorts in the van, and Grand Inquisitors trotting up behind with the baggage-train, would be lost in the knowledge that there was no

Moscow to return to, no Kremlin to give orders to its new puppets. Not only Moscow, not only the Kremlin would be gone, but the whole political structure which has kept the Russian people in slavery would be disrupted. Whatever illusion of victorious gain wars of the past may have presented to power-drunk autocrats, it is visible now, even to the fool and the criminal, that nothing is to be gained by a deliberately provoked atomic war.

Shortly before he died in 1895 Louis Pasteur was asked if he could see any way by which war could be abolished. He replied that there was only one way, but that this way was certain. War would abolish itself. It would become so devastating that it would become impossible. No doubt he was thinking of bacteriological war, but atomic war has got there first. It is because, and only because, the Kremlin sees no credit balance in an atomic war that it is so desperately anxious to ban the atom bomb. It wants to get back to the old kind of war, for which it has in full measure the material, the will, and the illusion of profit. It is peace from the determent of the atom bomb which is the sole object of its Peace Crusade. The strategics of the atom bomb are not that bombs in one place make up for a deficiency of tanks in another; nor that we are only safe so long as we have a superiority in them of x to one; nor that it is a retaliatory weapon as gas was in the last war, only to be used if the other side uses it first. The atom bomb is a weapon, not for victory in war, not for 'pairing' with the enemy in war, but to prevent war. To be prepared so to use it demands courage: the courage Samson showed when he pulled down the pillars of the temple. Samson sacrificed himself by making it perfectly clear now that the next war will be an atomic war: that, without regard to the atom bombs Russia may have, or her intention, or lack of intention, to use them, at the first movement of Communist troops against any country in the West, Moscow will be wiped out: we shall take the risk of sacrificing ourselves. It is a small risk compared with the certainty of war otherwise; a cheaply-bought risk for those of us who would far sooner die under an atom bomb than live under the Kremlin.

Unfortunately there are many good people, both in Britain and, more importantly, in America, who cannot bring themselves to accept the atom bomb as within the limits of what they call 'legitimate warfare'. Perhaps because I became a Pacifist on impersonal grounds, before I had experienced the horrors or even the discomforts of war, I consider all war, from the wars of the Israelites onwards, to be horrible, and all weapons of war, from the sword and the club and the spear onwards, to be barbarous. Every distinction between weapons of war as legitimate and illegitimate, as acceptable by, or repugnant to, humanity, is one more admission that war itself is acceptable and legitimate, so long as it is conducted in some fashion hallowed by previous exercise. If war is to be abolished, it will not be abolished by pretending that one method of killing is pleasing to God, and another displeasing; by accepting gratefully 200 raids with ordinary bombs which kill 1,000 'civilians' apiece, and exhibiting sanctimonious horror at one raid with an atomic bomb which kills the same number of 'civilians', and spares 20,000 airmen's lives.

I put the civilians into inverted commas to show that they have not yet got into uniform. I have never understood why the death of a clerk, a ploughman or a poet calls for a greater compassion from man, and a severer condemnation from God, if he should still be wearing his ordinary clothes. The object of aggressive war (however wrong) is to impose the national will upon another nation by the destruction of so much of its resources, human and material, that it can defend itself no longer. The object of defensive war (however right) is to resist that imposition by an even greater destruction of the enemy's resources, human and material. The human resources of a nation are every man, woman and child belonging to it. Yes, even children. Children in 1939 were young men and women in 1945, serving their country.

For war is hell, and it is not possible to contract out of all responsibility for hell by a high-minded disapproval of one particular mode of torture; nor would it be edifying to single out for disapproval the mode which particularly threatened oneself. A conscience which is outraged by the atom bomb should have been outraged long ago by war; for war has never made careful selection of its victims, nor been restrained by their number. A war to resist Communism would not be a game to be played under arbitrary rules, with certain approved weapons of a carefully limited range of destruction; it would be a life-and-death struggle, in which the West would only be engaged because it believed that there were higher values at stake than human lives.

Even the lives of its last man, woman and child. Even the lives of the enemy.

– In Summary –

C onsider the last war.

Austria (to *Servia*): Stop it, or I'll make you.

Russia (to *Austria*): Stop it, or I'll make you.

Germany (to *Russia*): Stop it, or I'll make you.

France (to *Germany*): Stop it, or I'll make you.

Germany (to *France*): Stop saying stop it, or I'll make you.

England (to *Germany*): Stop it, or I'll make you.

This reads like something from a comic opera, but it is exactly what happened.

A Twitch Upon the Thread: Writers on Fishing
Introduced by Jon Day

The best fishing writing is never only about fishing and the writers collected use angling as a way to write about love, loss, faith, and obsession. Includes contributions from Virginia Woolf, Charles Dickens, Arthur Ransome, Jerome K. Jerome, and more.

On Dolls
Edited by Kenneth Gross

The essays in this collection explore the seriousness of play and the mysteries of inanimate life: 'the unknown spaces, noises, dust, lost objects, and small animals that fill any house'. Includes contributions from Baudelaire, Rilke, Kafka and Freud.

On Christmas: A Seasonal Anthology
Introduced by Gyles Brandreth

A selection of Christmas-themed writings to savour during the highs and lows of Christmas Day. Includes selections from writers old and new, including Dostoevsky, Dickens, A. A. Milne, C. S. Lewis, and Ali Smith.

*All titles are available in the UK, and some titles are available in the rest of the world. For more information please visit www. nottinghilleditions.com.

A selection of our titles is distributed in the US and Canada by New York Review Books. For more information on available titles please visit www.nyrb.com